Robert Patterson

A Narrative of the Campaign in the Valley of the Shenandoah in 1861

Robert Patterson

A Narrative of the Campaign in the Valley of the Shenandoah in 1861

ISBN/EAN: 9783337425333

Printed in Europe, USA, Canada, Australia, Japan

Cover: Foto ©ninafisch / pixelio.de

More available books at **www.hansebooks.com**

A NARRATIVE

OF THE

CAMPAIGN

IN THE

Valley of the Shenandoah,

IN

1861.

BY ROBERT PATTERSON,

LATE MAJOR-GENERAL OF VOLUNTEERS.

FIFTH THOUSAND.

PHILADELPHIA:
JOHN CAMPBELL.
1865.

TO THE

GALLANT MEN

WHO SERVED UNDER MY COMMAND,
AND WHO WERE THE FIRST TO TAKE UP ARMS
AT THE CALL OF THEIR COUNTRY.

I Dedicate

THE FOLLOWING NARRATIVE OF THE

CAMPAIGN OF 1861.

NARRATIVE.

It has long been my desire to lay before the public the facts and documents which explain the operations of the forces under my command in the campaign of 1861. The misapprehensions, the misrepresentations which obtained currency in the absence of correct information on the subject, strongly prompted me to supply it, in justice to myself and to those who served with me. I have, however, been delayed in doing so by public considerations to which I will presently advert; but as they have, by lapse of time, lost the force that was attributed to them, I now feel myself at liberty to make a brief but well-attested contribution to the earlier history of the war.

On the 25th of July, 1861, the term of the three months' troops from Pennsylvania, whom I commanded, having expired, I was relieved from the command of my Department in Virginia, and, having been honorably discharged from the military service of the United States, returned to civil life.

The arms of the country had recently met with a severe disaster at Bull Run, and the public, whose expectation of success had been of the most sanguine character, were correspondingly depressed. Although conscious that I had executed, as far as lay in my power, every order that I had received, and was in no degree responsible for a disaster that I could not prevent, I was not surprised that I, as well as every other officer holding any command of importance at the time, should be the object of popular clamor. I was quite satisfied, however, to await the returning sense of the people, and to abide by their decision, when the natural passion and disappointment of the hour should pass away, and a full knowledge of the facts should enable them to form an intelligent and dispassionate judgment. This would very surely and certainly have come about, had it not been the interest of a great many persons in authority that the truth should not be known, and that no fair judgment of the cause of the disaster should be arrived at by the public.

It was of course desirable for those who had directed the movements at Bull Run to refer their defeat, if possible, to an occurrence for which they were not responsible, and not allow it to be attributed to any want of foresight or military skill on their part. The theory, therefore, that it was Johnston's unexpected arrival with reinforcements that lost them the battle, for which I was entirely responsible, answered the purpose exactly, was most ingenious, and highly gratifying to the wounded self-love of the army and the country.

The only drawback to the theory was that it was untrue. The truth is, I could not hold Johnston in the position where they had placed me, and they knew it. His arrival was not unexpected, for I had apprised them of it; and his coming did not cause the loss of the battle, as I can show by the testimony of the most distinguished soldiers who were present at it.

In determining upon the best mode of repelling these charges, bearing a semi-official character, I deemed it wise to consult with some of the regular officers of high distinction, who had served under me, and in whose judgment I had always placed great reliance. Major-General George H. Thomas, who had held a command under me, and whose subsequent brilliant career has justified the high opinion I was then led to entertain of him, writes to a mutual friend as follows:

"CAMP NEAR HYATTSTOWN, MD.,
August 25, 1861.

"DEAR COLONEL:

"Your note has just been handed me. I had a conversation with Newton yesterday on the subject of General Patterson's campaign. He was on the eve of writing to the General, and asked me what he should state was my opinion as to the General's course. I told him that he could say that, if I were situated as he was, I would make a statement of all the facts to the General-in-chief, or the Secretary of War, fortifying it with copies of the orders, &c., and demand justice at their hands, and, if they were not disposed to give it, I would then demand a court of inquiry.

"Yours truly,
"GEO. H. THOMAS.

"P. S. I think, however, that time will set the General all right, as I see the papers are much more favorable to him than at first."

General John Newton and General Fitz-John Porter both concurring that the course indicated by General Thomas was the true one, and that a newspaper controversy was both an improper and unsoldierly way of setting myself right, I addressed the following letter to the Secretary of War, after I supposed that a sufficient time had elapsed to prevent any information derived from an investigation being of detriment to the public service (*Report Committee on Conduct of the War*, vol. ii, p. 114):

"PHILADELPHIA, PENNSYLVANIA,
November 1, 1861.
"SIR:

"Believing to the present moment that, on account of other persons, a public examination into the manner in which the affairs of the Department of Pennsylvania, while under my command, were conducted, and the publication of the correspondence with, and orders to me of the General-in-chief, especially connected with the late campaign in Maryland and Virginia, might be detrimental to the interests of the service, I have refrained from asking for an investigation or permission to publish the orders by which I was controlled.

"The same reason has caused me studiously to avoid verbal statements on the subject, in reply to numerous inquiries.

"Charges have been made publicly through the press, and the impression created, that the design of the campaign was not carried out by me, but rather deranged by my neglect or violation of orders.

"Intimations against my loyalty have been insidiously circulated.

"From the silence of my immediate commander, I infer he does not design to relieve me from the odium attached to these reports and rumors.

"While I am willing, if the general good demand it, to suffer personally, and am desirous that no course on my part shall prove injurious to public interests, yet I believe the time has arrived when the question as to the manner in which I executed the duties intrusted to me may be fully investigated with safety, so that the failure to accomplish certain results, never anticipated of my command by the General-in-chief until he saw his defeat, may be ascribed to the real cause.

"Further silence on my part would confirm the impression that I plead guilty to the charges against my honor, my loyalty, and my military capacity. I have a right at least to be relieved from the position in which my long silence, caused solely by an earnest desire for the success of our cause, has left me.

"In presenting this my application for a court of inquiry, or permission to publish my correspondence with the General-in-chief, I claim, and am now ready to substantiate,

"1st. That if the General-in-chief ever designed my command to enter upon the soil of Virginia with prospect of success, he destroyed my power when greatest, and when that of the enemy was weakest, by recalling to Washington, after they had crossed the Potomac, all my regular troops, with the Rhode Island regiment and battery, leaving me but a single company of cavalry, which had not then been one month in service, and entirely destitute of artillery.

"2d. The General-in-chief forbade my advance, and compelled me to recall to Maryland all the troops which, confident of success, had crossed the Potomac into Virginia, in execution of a plan which had been submitted to him and had received his cordial approbation.

"3d. That for a long time the General-in-chief kept my command in a crippled condition, and demanded my advance after he had withdrawn from me all my available artillery, and only after the enemy had had time to become vastly my superior in artillery, infantry, and cavalry, and was intrenched. In answer to my earnest appeals, he reinforced me only after the occasion for employing reinforcements had passed away.

"4th. That if the General-in-chief designed me to do

more than threaten the enemy at Winchester, he did not divulge his wish.

"5th. That if the General-in-chief expected me to follow to Manassas 'close upon the heels of Johnston,' he expected a physical impossibility; the enemy moving part of the way by rail, from an intermediate point, and my army on foot, entering an enemy's country, and guarding a heavy train, and a depot retained by him in an improper place.

"6th. The General-in-chief forbade pursuit of the enemy, in the event that he should retire towards Manassas, fearing to press him on Washington.

"7th. That I was informed by the General-in-chief that the attack on Manassas would be made on Tuesday, the 16th of July, instead of Sunday, the 21st, at which time he directed me to make such a demonstration upon Winchester as to keep the enemy at that place. I claim that the demonstration was made on that day, and that he did not avail himself of the fruits of that movement, as he had expected to do. All that was demanded of me, and more, was effected.

"8th. That if the army I commanded had attacked Winchester on Tuesday, the 16th of July, as it has since been claimed I was ordered to do, two armies instead of one would have been demoralized, and the enemy would have turned with all the flush of victory to a triumph in front of Washington.

"9th. That I have suffered additional injustice at the hands of the General-in-chief, who sanctioned and fixed the impression that the enemy at Winchester was inferior to me in force in every arm of the service, and yet has not corrected the report, although he knew, two days after the Battle of Bull Run, that siege artillery, three times as numerous, and heavier than mine, had been left by the enemy at Winchester, while a greater number of guns had been carried away.

"Very respectfully, your obedient servant,

"R. PATTERSON,
"Major-General."

This application was acknowledged as follows:

"WAR DEPARTMENT,
WASHINGTON, November 3, 1861.

"DEAR SIR:

"I have the honor to acknowledge the receipt of your letter, bearing date November 1. The Secretary of War is absent on a visit North. I will forward it to him by this day's mail, and ask for instructions.

"Very respectfully,
"THOMAS A. SCOTT,
"Ass't Secretary of War.

"GENERAL R. PATTERSON,
"Philadelphia."

After waiting a reasonable time for an answer to my application, I again appealed to the Secretary of War, as follows:

"PHILADELPHIA, November 26, 1861.

"SIR:

"I respectfully request that you will do me the justice to refer to my letter of the 1st instant, and give it your early attention. I cannot refrain from intimating a confident hope that my application for a court of inquiry will meet with your favorable consideration, and that an order for the detail will be made at the earliest moment consistent with the interests of the service.

"I have the honor to be, with great respect,
"Your obedient servant,
"R. PATTERSON,
"Major-General.

"HON. SIMON CAMERON,
"Secretary of War."

This brought me the following refusal of my application:

"WAR DEPARTMENT, November 30, 1861.

"GENERAL:

"I have to acknowledge the receipt of your letter of the 26th instant, calling my attention to your communication of the 1st November, which contains a request for an inquiry into the late campaign in Virginia, in which you commanded a part of the United States forces.

"Your letter did not reach me until my return to this city, and subsequent to the departure of Lieutenant-General Scott for Europe.

"There appears to have been no precedent in our service for an investigation or trial of an officer's conduct after he has received an honorable discharge. The inquiry you desire to have instituted would equally concern the late General-in-chief, and, as it appears to me, in justice to him, should not be made in his absence.

"The respect I have always entertained for you, as well as the friendly relations which have long existed between us, would claim for any personal request from you the most prompt and favorable attention; but, in my public capacity, in the present condition of affairs, I cannot convince myself that my duty to the Government and to the country would justify me in acceding to your request. I must, therefore, reluctantly decline the appointment of a court of inquiry at this time.

"With much respect, your obedient servant,
"SIMON CAMERON,
"Secretary of War.
"GENERAL R. PATTERSON,
"Philadelphia, Penna."

The voyage of the General-in-chief to Europe was, of course, as unexpected to me as it was to the public at large, although the additional insinuation was made against me that I had taken advantage of his absence to make my request for a trial. The receipt of my letter asking an investigation was, however, fortunately acknowledged before he left the country, and his speedy return removed at least one reason for refusing to allow me to be heard. Determined to persevere and obtain an investigation, if possible, I went to Washington and called at the War Department, had a long interview with the Secretary, General Cameron, and the Assistant Secretary, Hon. T. A. Scott, showed the orders and correspondence, and insisted on an investigation. Both admitted that the official orders and correspondence as presented placed the case in a very different light from their previous understanding of it. Mr. Scott said I ought to have a court, in order that justice might be done to me and all others interested in the matter. To this the Secretary assented, but said that a court would throw the blame on General Scott, and this he would never consent to; that General Scott had now retired from the service full of years and full of honors; that he desired him to pass the remainder of his life in repose, enjoying, as he deserved, the gratitude of the whole country; and that no consideration on earth would induce him to do any act that would plant a thorn in General Scott's pillow. To all this I cordially assented, adding that there was no man living I more honored and venerated than General Scott, and that, it it were simply a question between General Scott and myself as to who should bear the blame, if the blame rested with either, I would be willing to bear it, and go down to the grave with it; but that I had children and grandchildren and warm friends, and it was due to them, and to Pennsylvania, whose officer I was, as well as to the troops I commanded, that the truth should be made manifest; that I must have a trial, or an official order or letter referring to my services and approving them. To this General Cameron assented, and promised to give one, but, unfortunately for me, before it was given, circumstances occurred which induced him to leave the Cabinet, after which he could not issue an order. At the close of the interview, General Cameron said he would like the President to see the official orders and correspondence, to which I replied that I desired this exceedingly. Mr. Scott offered to see the President at once. He did so. The President fixed 7½ o'clock in the evening, at the Executive Mansion. I called at that hour, was most kindly received, and read the orders and correspondence, to which the President attentively listened. When I had finished, and after some conversation, the President addressed me in nearly the following words: "General Patterson, I have never found fault with or censured you; I have never been able to see that you could have done anything else than you did do. Your hands were tied; you obeyed orders, and did your duty, and I am satisfied with your conduct." This was said with a manner so frank, so candid, and so manly, as to secure my respect, confidence, and good will. I expressed to the President my great gratification with, and tendered my sincere thanks for, his fairness towards me, and his courtesy in hearing my case, and giving me some five hours of his time. I said that so far as he and the War Department were concerned I was satisfied, but that I must have a court and a trial by my peers, in order to have a public approval of my conduct, and stop the abuse daily lavished upon me. The President replied that he would cheerfully accede to any practicable measure to do me justice, but that I need not expect to escape abuse as long as I was of any importance or value to the community, adding that he received infinitely more abuse than I did, but he had ceased to regard it, and I must learn to do the same.

My next application for redress was to Congress. At my request, Mr. Sherman offered the following resolution in the Senate of the United States (*Report*, p. 117, No. 3):

"SENATE OF THE UNITED STATES,
December 17, 1861.

" On motion of Mr. Sherman,

" *Resolved*, That the Secretary of War be requested, if not incompatible with the public interests, to furnish the Senate with copies of the correspondence between Lieutenant-General Scott and Major-General Patterson, with all orders from the former to the latter, from the 16th day of April, 1861, to the 25th day of July, inclusive."

To this resolution of the Senate, unanimously adopted, the following response was made:

"WAR DEPARTMENT, December 24, 1861.

" SIR:

" In answer to a resolution of the Senate of the 17th instant, I have the honor to transmit herewith a report of the Adjutant-General, from which it will be perceived that it is not deemed compatible with the public interest at this time to furnish the correspondence between Generals Scott and Patterson, as called for.

" Very respectfully, your obedient servant,
" SIMON CAMERON,
"Secretary of War.

"HON. H. HAMLIN,
"President of the Senate."

"Headquarters of the Army,
Adjutant-General's Office, Washington,
December 23, 1861.

"Sir:

"In compliance with your instructions, I have the honor to report that, after due consideration, the General-in-chief is of the opinion it would be 'incompatible with the public interest to furnish the Senate with copies of the correspondence between Lieutenant-General Scott and Major-General Patterson, and with all orders from the former to the latter from the 16th day of April, 1861, to the 25th day of July, inclusive,' as called for in the Senate resolution of December 17th, 1861.

"I am, sir, very respectfully, your obedient servant,

"L. Thomas,
"Adjutant-General.

"Hon. Secretary of War."

Had a court of inquiry been allowed me, no publication of the orders or correspondence would have been necessary. The court would have investigated the case, and if it had appeared that I had obeyed my orders and done my duty, they would have said so. I would have been satisfied, and there the case would have terminated.

The refusal to publish my correspondence and orders, being put upon the ground "that it was not deemed compatible with the public interest," not only deprived me of their official publication, but debarred me from publishing them in any other way, although I was daily the subject of attack, upon points which they would instantly have refuted. I was thus placed in a position in which I could be attacked with perfect impunity, while any answer by myself would have rendered me liable to the reproach of publishing what the highest military authorities deemed detrimental to the public service. I therefore bore, and have borne without a word of reply, the absurd calumnies that have been heaped upon me. Nothing was too gross for popular belief. It was even asserted as a fact beyond all doubt, that General Joseph E. Johnston who commanded the forces opposing me, and with whom I had no connection or relationship, was my brother-in-law, and it is probably now credited everywhere out of Philadelphia.

The facts which I have stated, certainly prove that I had no desire to avoid an investigation of my official conduct, but that I was then, as I am now, not only willing but anxious to meet frankly and fairly any allegation that could be made against me. That I had been honorably discharged from the service of my country, was not, as it might have been, put forward by me as a reason why I should not ask for an investigation, but was the excuse given by the Government for not granting it. Having by an honorable discharge declared they had no fault to find with me, they said that no court they could grant me could do any more.

I certainly think, therefore, I can claim that I was justified by those who had full knowledge of what I had done, and full authority to rebuke me had I done wrong.

The day after the War Department had declined to furnish the Senate with copies of the correspondence and orders received by me from the Commander-in-chief, as being detrimental to the public interests, a Committee of Congress on the "Conduct of the War" began an investigation of the circumstances attending the Battle of Bull Run, including my operations. This struck me as somewhat inconsistent, but the suggestion did not then occur to me that the object was, by a Star Chamber proceeding, to prepare a report setting all fair play and truth at defiance. This too plainly appeared subsequently. At the time I was much gratified, supposing, of course, that the investigation would be full, fair, and candid. I need hardly say, in addressing American citizens, that in a question involving all that is dear to a man or an officer, I expected to be confronted with any witness who should testify against me. I presumed that I should be allowed to cross-examine them. I supposed that at least my own witnesses would be examined. Not so, however, did it appear to this Honorable Committee. I never was allowed to hear the evidence of a single witness. I never was permitted to have a copy of any testimony affecting my character or conduct. I was refused the privilege of having examined the witnesses I deemed most material. Even the following questions, left with the Committee, certainly unobjectionable, which I requested, if not myself permitted to be present, might be asked by the Committee, appear by the published testimony never to have been put to a single witness:

1. Were you with General Patterson's column in July last? If so, in what capacity?

2. Did or did not General Patterson possess the respect and confidence of his officers and men?

3. What was the effect on General Patterson's army of the order of the Commander-in-chief directing him to send to Washington all his regular troops, with the Rhode Island regiment and battery, and the consequent recross-

ing of the Potomac by that part of the army which had entered Virginia?

4. Was General Patterson's movement from Martinsburg by Bunker Hill and Charlestown, on the 15th, 16th, and 17th of July, in your judgment, judicious or otherwise, and were this and his other movements well conducted or otherwise?

5. Which do you consider the better strategic point, Martinsburg or Charlestown?

6. What at that time, according to your knowledge and information, was the relative strength in men and guns, of the armies of General Patterson and General Johnston?

7. Did you then or do you now think that General Patterson ought to have attacked General Johnston at Winchester, and if he had done so, what in your opinion would have been the probable result?

8. Was there any open opposition to a further advance by officers or men, and if so, where or when?

9. Did or did not General Patterson use his influence with the volunteers of his command, whose term of service was about to expire, to remain with him a week or ten days longer, to enable him to hold his position at Charlestown till reinforced with three-years men, or to obey any order he might receive from General Scott, and if so, what was the character of his appeal, and what was the response to it?

On the first day of my own examination, I said to the Committee, "If any testimony has been given that affects the management of my column, I would like to have it read before I begin. I believe it is customary to have that done." The Chairman in response to this said, " What Congress expects of us, is to obtain such facts as we suppose will be useful in throwing light upon the military operations of the army, in order to apply any remedy that may be necessary. I perceive by the documents that you have before you, that you are about entering upon what is a very minute narration: that might be necessary if you were accused; it might then be very proper." The Hon. Andrew Johnson here interfered, and on his motion I was allowed to proceed and make my statement, certainly under the impression that before the Committee, at least, to use the words of the Chairman, " I was not accused," and had therefore nothing to reply to.

It now appears from their Report, that the main portion of the testimony upon which they have relied to make out an accusation against me, was then in their possession, yet it was thus withheld from me, and it was only by the courtesy of Mr. Johnson that I was permitted to make a statement.

That it was not the intention of Congress that any committee of their body should so prostitute their functions, I sincerely believe. No stronger evidence can be given of their sense of the gross unfairness of the course pursued by this Committee than the resolution adopted in the House of Representatives in 1862, on the motion of Mr. Colfax.

Mr. Colfax's resolution was adopted,—yeas 90, nays 41. It is as follows:

"*Resolved*, That the course adopted by the Naval Investigating Committee of 1859, of communicating to the officers of the Government copies of the evidence apparently adverse to them, and giving them an opportunity to cross-examine the witnesses against them, or to refute or explain their testimony, is, in the opinion of this House, worthy of imitation, whenever practicable, by the investigating committees appointed by order of the House of Representatives, especially when the said committees receive and collect such testimony in secret session ; and that it is contrary to the plainest principles of justice to condemn any citizen upon *ex parte* evidence, taken against him by a committee in secret, and the purport of which has not, if practicable, been laid before him by the said committee, with an opportunity to explain or refute it before the report is made public."

Any body or committee seeking truth could hardly have acted otherwise. It is only those bent on making a report consonant with their own wishes, who could lose sight of all fairness and justice in effecting their purpose.

Since the Committee, in its published Report on the Battle of Bull Run, has endeavored to countenance the imputation of blame to me for "failure to hold the forces of Johnston in the Valley of the Shenandoah," I presume that I am at liberty, as I can no longer hope for a military investigation, to state my own case without detriment to the public interest. This I propose now to do.

On the 15th of April, 1861, the President, by proclamation, called for a military force of seventy-five thousand men, of which the quota assigned to Pennsylvania was at first sixteen (afterwards reduced to fourteen) regiments, to serve as infantry or riflemen, for the term of three months, unless sooner discharged. On the 16th, myself and the late Major-General W. H. Keim were selected by Governor Curtin as the Major-Generals to command the Pennsylvania troops.

On the same day, instantly relinquishing the large business in which I was engaged, I commenced organizing regiments for service in Philadelphia, with great and immediate success.

To use the words of the then Adjutant-General of our State:

"Pennsylvania not only furnished promptly her assigned quota of fourteen regiments, but increased the number to twenty-five, and such was the patriotic ardor of the people that the service of about thirty additional regiments had to be refused, making in all more than one-half the requisition of the President. Four days after this call, Pennsylvania had placed at the national capital six hundred men, the first to arrive for its defence, and ten days later the entire twenty-five regiments were organized and in the field."

While performing my part in this preparation, in which all were zealous and active, I was by the order of Lieutenant-General Scott, placed in command of "the Department of Washington," embracing the States of Pennsylvania, Delaware, and Maryland, and the District of Columbia, my headquarters being in Philadelphia. I was unceasingly occupied in organizing, equipping and forwarding troops for the defence of the city of Washington, in sustaining the Union feeling in Maryland and Delaware, and in the adoption of means to prevent one or both from seceding and joining the States in rebellion, also, in providing means for the defence and protection of the frontier of my Department, and of the Delaware River. My attention was also early engaged in opening a route to Washington via Annapolis, for which purpose I sent the Hon. John Sherman of Ohio, one of my aides-de-camp, to General Scott, with a despatch pointing out the advantage of the Annapolis route at that time.

My suggestion was adopted, and the Annapolis route approved. Pending this, I had ordered Brigadier-General B. F. Butler with a Massachusetts regiment to proceed to Annapolis, in a steamboat patriotically furnished for the purpose by S. M. Felton, Esq., President of the Philadelphia, Wilmington and Baltimore Railroad Company. General Butler was ordered to hold Annapolis, to employ the regiments as they arrived there in opening the way to Washington, to seize the Annapolis Junction, to station a competent force there, and guard the whole line of road thoroughly. These services he rendered in conformity with my orders.

Having succeeded in securing a well-protected line of communication with Washington, I turned my attention to re-establishing the route through Baltimore, and compelling the turbulent spirits of that city to submit to lawful authority, and in this I was well aided by his Excellency Governor Hicks. The troops to force a passage through Baltimore, were the First Regiment Pennsylvania Volunteer Artillery (Seventeenth of the line), and Sherman's Battery, the whole under command of my son, the late General Francis E. Patterson.

It is due to the officers and men of this command to say, that their entrance into and passage through Baltimore, was an encouraging exhibition of Union determination.

I had been deeply convinced that the contest upon which we were entering was very much underrated by our rulers, and that the three months' troops, though very well for the moment, should not be our sole dependence for carrying on operations of the magnitude which I thought that I foresaw.

I felt that if advantage was not taken of the time which their service gave us to prepare for the future, we should find ourselves at some critical moment with all our troops going out of service and none coming in to replace them.

The interruption of all communication with Washington left me, in the absence of orders, to rely wholly upon my own judgment as commander of the Department, and I then took a step by which I incurred very great responsibility; and, although I received the implied censure of the War Department by their revocation of my order, as soon as they were able to communicate with the North, yet I have never regretted it, and I confidently appeal to subsequent events to justify my action.

On the 25th of April I addressed the following letter to the Governor of Pennsylvania:

"HEADQUARTERS
MILITARY DEPARTMENT OF WASHINGTON,
PHILADELPHIA, April 25th, 1861.

"SIR:

"I feel it my duty to express to you my clear and decided opinion that the force at the disposal of this Department should be increased without delay.

"I, therefore, have to request your Excellency to direct that twenty-five additional regiments of infantry and one regiment of cavalry be called for forthwith, to be mustered into the service of the United States.

"Officers will be detailed to inspect and muster the men into service as soon as I am informed of the points of rendezvous which may be designated by your Excellency.

"I have the honor to be, with great respect,
"Your obedient servant,
"R. PATTERSON,
"Major-General.

"HIS EXCELLENCY ANDREW G. CURTIN,
"Governor of Pennsylvania."

The Governor, with his usual promptness, responded to this appeal, and had actually raised a large body of men, when the War Department declined to indorse my call. On the contrary, they would not enlarge their first requisition to cover the regiments already in the field from Pennsylvania, but stated "that it was more important to reduce than enlarge the number."

In spite of this rebuff, I determined to make one more effort to obtain at least some troops "for the war" while they had the disposition to enlist for that term. With this view, I sent to the Secretary of War my aide-de-camp, the Hon. John Sherman, Senator from Ohio, who had done me the honor of serving on my staff, hoping that his well-known character for patriotism and ability might add weight to my views, and induce the Secretary to modify his determination, and permit me to secure at least three of my finest regiments, who were willing to remain and re-enlist. But in vain, as the following letter will show:

"WASHINGTON, May 30, 1861.
"MY DEAR GENERAL:
"I have had, as you suggested, an interview with the

Secretary of War. He says he cannot now accept any more regiments for the war; that no doubt the three years' men will be needed, but that the question of their acceptance for the war cannot be decided until near the expiration of their present enlistment. I feel very well assured that if the aspect of affairs is not materially changed that these regiments will be accepted, if within the next month they justify your confidence in them.

"The Secretary informs me that the two New York regiments now at Harrisburg will be left under your command.

"I write in great haste to send by present opportunity.

"With great respect,
"JOHN SHERMAN.
"MAJOR-GENERAL R. PATTERSON."

The Executive of Pennsylvania fortunately took a broader view of the subject, and induced the Legislature to pass an act to take into the service of the State the men whom, at my request, he had commenced raising for the United States. In his messege of 1862 he says:

"Men more than sufficient in number to form some ten regiments of the Reserve Corps had, previous to the 15th of May, been accepted by me in pursuance of a call on me (afterwards rescinded) for twenty-five regiments, and were then already assembled and subject to my control. Most of these men volunteered for the Reserve Corps, and were immediately organized."

This was the origin of the famous Reserve Corps of Pennsylvania, which was so gladly taken into the service of the United States immediately after the Battle of Bull Run, and by its prompt transfer from Harrisburg to Washington, gave security to the national capital.

Of their glorious after career, it is not necessary for me to speak; it forms one of the brightest pages in the history of the war. Had they been accepted by the Government when I asked for them, they could have been ready for the movement of General McDowell, and twenty-five thousand three years' troops would thus have been added to his force. If added to my column, I could have left the Pennsylvania border amply protected on my advance, and could have joined battle without violating my instructions, to be "in superior or equal force," and with every prospect of a brilliant result.

Having established order in Baltimore and secured free communication with Washington, my attention was next turned to the recapture of Harper's Ferry, then held by the rebels under General Joseph E. Johnston.

To accomplish this a camp was formed at Chambersburg, under the late Major-General W. H. Keim. On the 2d of June I left Philadelphia and took command in person of the troops at Chambersburg, intending to carry out a plan previously submitted to and approved by General Scott, to attack and capture or disperse the enemy at Harper's Ferry. On the 4th of June I was forbidden to advance until certain reinforcements were sent me. The order was as follows:

"HEADQUARTERS OF THE ARMY,
WASHINGTON, June 4, 1861.

"MAJOR-GENERAL PATTERSON, U. S. A.,
Chambersburg, Pa.

"General Scott says, do not make a move forward until you are joined by a battery of the Fourth (4th) Artillery and a battalion of five (5) companies Third U. S. Infantry, to leave here the 6th inst. for Carlisle. Company F, Fourth Artillery, is the one to be mounted.

"Orders have been given to purchase horses and collect the guns, equipments, &c., as soon as possible, at Carlisle. It will require some days, but the General considers this addition to your force indispensable. If two (2) Ohio regiments come to you, retain them.

"Also halt the first two (2) regiments that may pass through Harrisburg from the North to this city and add them to your force. You will receive a letter from the General before you move.

"E. D. TOWNSEND,
"Asst. Adjt. Genl."

The following is the letter of instruction referred to (see *Report*, vol. ii, p. 118):

"HEADQUARTERS OF THE ARMY,
WASHINGTON, June 8, 1861.

"SIR:

"I think your expedition against Harper's Ferry well projected, and that success in it would be an important step in the war. But there must be no reverse. Hence I have given you the best reinforcements within my reach, and have just ordered Colonel Burnside's fine Rhode Island regiment of infantry with its battery (about twelve hundred strong) to proceed to Carlisle and there receive your orders. A company of the Fourth Artillery (to receive its horses and battery at Carlisle), with the battalion of the Third Infantry, took the same route, and with the same instructions, yesterday. This battery may not be ready for you in time. These heavy rains must swell the Potomac and delay your passage some days. I am organizing to aid you a small secondary expedition under Colonel Stone. He will have about twenty-five hundred men, including two troops of cavalry and a section (two pieces) of artillery.

"The movements by road and canal will commence the 10th inst., and, passing up the country (touching at Rockville), be directed upon the ferry opposite Leesburg. This may be but a diversion in your favor, but possibly it may be turned into an effective co-operation. Colonel Stone will be instructed to open a communication with you, if practicable, and you will make a corresponding effort on your part. I do not distinctly foresee that we shall be able to make any diversion in your behalf on the other side of the Potomac, beyond repairing the lower part of the railroad leading from Alexandria towards the Manassas Gap.

"I have said that we must sustain no reverse; but this is not enough: a check or a drawn battle would be a victory to the enemy, filling his heart with joy, his ranks with men, and his magazines with voluntary contributions.

"Take your measures, therefore, circumspectly; make a good use of your engineers and other experienced staff officers and generals, and attempt nothing without a clear prospect of success, as you will find the enemy strongly posted and not inferior to you in numbers.

"With entire confidence in your valor and judgment,
"I remain your brother soldier,
"WINFIELD SCOTT.

"MAJOR-GENERAL PATTERSON,
"United States Forces."

When General Johnston perceived that I was about to cross the Potomac, he abandoned Harper's Ferry and retreated towards Bunker Hill.

On the next day my forces commenced crossing the Potomac in pursuit. Part of my forces were on one side of the river and part on the other, all in the highest state of confidence and excitement, when I received a telegraphic despatch to send "all the regular troops, horse and foot, and the Rhode Island regiment, to Washington."

"WASHINGTON, June 16, 1861.

"What movement, if any, in pursuit of the enemy, do you propose to make consequent on the evacuation of

Harper's Ferry? If no pursuit, and I recommend none, specifically, send to me, at once, all the regular troops, horse and foot, with you, and the Rhode Island regiment.

"WINFIELD SCOTT.
"MAJOR-GENERAL PATTERSON."

In my response to this despatch, I said (*Report*, vol. ii, p. 122), "To-day and to-morrow about 9000 will cross to Virginia, there to await transportation, and to be sent forward in detachments well sustained;" and I requested that "the regulars be permitted to remain for the present," and I submitted my desire, "first, to transfer to Harper's Ferry my base of operations, depots, headquarters, &c.; second, to open and maintain free communication east and west along the Baltimore and Ohio Railroad; third, to hold at Harper's Ferry, Martinsburg, and Charlestown, a strong force, gradually and securely advancing, as they are prepared, portions towards Winchester, &c., and operate with the column in the third proposition towards Woodstock, and cut off all communication with the west. We will thus force the enemy to retire, and recover without a struggle a conquered country," &c. I also added, "If I am permitted to carry out this plan, the Baltimore and Ohio Railroad and Canal will be in operation in a week, and a free line to St. Louis established." In answer to this the General-in-chief telegraphed to me:

"WASHINGTON, June 16, 1861.

"Why a detachment upon Winchester? If strong enough, the detachment would drive the enemy from Winchester, Strasburg, and Manassas Junction, or perhaps from Winchester via Staunton, towards Richmond. What would be the gain by driving the enemy on either of these places? And if your detachment be not strong, it would be lost. Hence the detachment, if not bad, would be useless. The enemy is concentrating upon Arlington and Alexandria, and this is the line to be looked to. Is Wallace, at Cumberland, threatened from below? If so, the threatening detachment is cut off by your passage of the Potomac. McClellan has been told to-day, to send nothing across the mountains to support you, since the evacuation of Harper's Ferry. You are strong enough without. The regulars with you are most needed here; send them and the Rhode Island regiment as fast as disengaged. Keep within the above limits until you can satisfy me you ought to go beyond them. Report frequently.

"WINFIELD SCOTT.

"MAJOR-GENERAL PATTERSON, Commanding."

"WASHINGTON, June 16, 1861.

"You tell me you arrived last night at Hagerstown, and McClellan writes you are checked at Harper's Ferry. Where are you?

"WINFIELD SCOTT.

"MAJOR-GENERAL PATTERSON, Commanding."

"HEADQUARTERS OF THE ARMY,
WASHINGTON, July 17, 1861.

"To GENERAL PATTERSON:

"We are pressed here. Send the troops I have twice called for, without delay.

"WINFIELD SCOTT."

This last was imperative, and the troops were sent, leaving me without a single piece of artillery, and for the time with but one troop of cavalry, which had not been in service over a month. Of this recall General Cadwalader, in his testimony before the Committee on the Conduct of the War, thus speaks:

"Answer. My division, as a part of General Patterson's

column, was in the advance. I crossed the Potomac from Williamsport, and when Johnston retreated, as we advanced upon Harper's Ferry, we went down as far as Falling Waters, on the Virginia side.

"I was there met with an order to send to Washington all the regular troops—they were all under my command—as it was thought that Johnston had fallen back to reinforce Beauregard, and that Washington was in danger. All the regular troops being ordered to Washington, and the object of dislodging the enemy from Harper's Ferry having been accomplished, General Patterson was compelled, or rather induced, to give me the order to fall back. I was then on the way to Martinsburg, and had got as far as Falling Waters, some miles on the other side of the Potomac. General Patterson was still at Hagerstown. A great misfortune, by-the-by, was that recall."

The Hon. John Sherman, in a letter addressed to me, dated August 30, 1861, gives it as his judgment that "the great error of General Scott undoubtedly was, that he gave way to a causeless apprehension that Washington was to be attacked before the meeting of Congress, and therefore weakened you when you were advancing. No subsequent movement could repair that error." This I venture to say, will be the conclusion of any one who dispassionately examines the subject. I was mortified and humiliated at having to recross the river without striking a blow. I knew that my reputation would be grievously damaged by it; the country could not understand the meaning of this crossing and recrossing, this marching and countermarching in face of the foe, and that I would be censured without stint for such apparent vacillation and want of purpose. In this I was not mistaken, for not only the public, but persons in "the highest military positions" at Washington, did great injustice to me and my command. I was criticized, too, for not doing, exactly what my own plan contemplated, and what I was actually carrying out, when forced to return to this side of the Potomac by the action of the General-in-chief. Of this I was informed in the subjoined letter from the Hon. John Sherman.

"WASHINGTON, June 30, 1861.
"MY DEAR SIR:
. . . . "Great injustice is done you and your command here, and by persons in the highest military positions. I have been asked over and over again why you did not push on to Martinsburg, Harper's Ferry, and Winchester. I have been restrained by my being on your staff from saying more than simply, that you executed your orders, and that when you were prepared to advance your best troops were recalled to Washington. . . . .
"Very truly, yours,
"JOHN SHERMAN.
"MAJOR-GENERAL R. PATTERSON."

On the 20th of June, the General-in-chief asked me "without delay to propose to him a plan of operations." On the 21st I submitted one, as follows (*Report*, vol. ii, p. 123):

"HEADQUARTERS DEPARTMENT OF PENNSYLVANIA,
HAGERSTOWN, MARYLAND, June 21, 1861.
"COLONEL:
"I have the honor to acknowledge the receipt of the telegram of the General-in-chief, calling for a plan of operations, with a portion of my force, to sweep the enemy from Leesburg, &c.
"Inclosed is a copy of my telegraphic reply. The following is my plan. To carry out the views of the General-in-chief, I propose,—
"1st. To occupy the Maryland Heights, with a brigade

(2100 men); fortify and arm with Doubleday's artillery; provision for 20 days, to secure against investment.

"2d. To move all supplies to Frederick, and immediately thereafter abandon this line of operations, threatening with a force to open a route through Harper's Ferry, this force to be the sustaining one for the command on Maryland Heights.

"3d. To send everything else available, horse, foot, and artillery, to cross the Potomac near Point of Rocks, and unite with Colonel Stone at Leesburg. From that point I can operate as circumstances shall demand and your orders require.

"If no blow is to be struck here, I think this change of position important to keep alive the ardor of our men, as well as to force an enemy. The reasons for this change of depot will be so apparent to the General-in-chief that I need not refer to them. By the employment of the local transportation of the country, I can soon make the necessary changes, and will hasten to carry out your orders.

"I have many reports in regard to the movements of the force opposite us in Virginia, and have reason to believe that when the regulars were withdrawn, General Johnston, with 13,000 men and 22 pieces of artillery, was marching to the attack, that night posted his forces, expecting an attack the following morning. I regret we did not meet the enemy, so confident am I that with this well-appointed force, the result would have been favorable to us, and that this portion of Virginia would now be peaceably occupied. Reports of the enemy having returned to Harper's Ferry, and driven the occupants to this shore, reached me yesterday. I immediately despatched a strong force to take the position in the vicinity of Sharpsburg, and protect all parties on this side of the river, and drive back any force which may attempt to cross.

"I am, Colonel, very respectfully,
"Your obedient servant,
"R. PATTERSON,
"Major-General, Commanding.

"COLONEL E. D. TOWNSEND,
"Assistant Adjutant-General U. S. Army, Washington, D. C."

Had this plan been adopted, the army of General McDowell and my own would have been precisely where they ought to have been. I would have been in a position to have aided General McDowell, and to have taken and torn up, if I could not have held, a portion of "the railroad leading from Manassas to the Valley of Virginia." This would not only have destroyed "the communications between the forces under Beauregard and those under Johnston," but it would have prevented either from throwing large reinforcements to the other when assailed.

And if I could not prevent Johnston from joining Beauregard, which I certainly could not do while stationed anywhere between Williamsport and Winchester, I could have joined McDowell in the attack on Manassas, and assailed and turned the enemy's left. Had my suggestions been adopted, the Battle of Bull Run might have been a victory, instead of a defeat.

It thus appears that, just one month before the Battle of Bull Run, knowing that I was upon a false line and could do no good there, I proposed to abandon it and go to Leesburg, where it is now admitted I ought to have been. The wisdom of this plan is singularly confirmed by the opinion of one of the ablest military writers and critics of the day, Major-General Halleck. In an article on "The Art of War," published in the New York Times, of the 22d of July, 1862, and written in entire ignorance of my having previously suggested the very course he recommends, he says:

"Patterson and McDowell's columns moved on exterior lines, leaving the armies of Johnston and Beauregard between them; they concentrated their forces at Bull Run and defeated McDowell's army, and might have done the same thing to the army of Patterson. *Had the latter crossed the Potomac at Leesburg, he would have threatened Johnston's communications much more effectually than at Martinsburg, and at the same time would have been near enough to McDowell to assist him, or to receive assistance from him, as circumstances might have required.*

"Johnston must then have abandoned Harper's Ferry and Winchester, and united with Beauregard, or the latter must have moved to the assistance of the former; for had they remained separated, both Patterson and McDowell could have moved between them.

"In that case, Beauregard must have fallen back towards Richmond, and Johnston must have been isolated. If Johnston had fallen back upon Manassas Junction (as in fact he did on the 21st day of July), Patterson would have been able to assist McDowell at the Battle of Bull Run; whereas, by his exterior line of operations he actually gained nothing. Newspaper critics have attempted to throw all the blame of this defeat upon Patterson, and have compared him to Grouchy at Waterloo. From all the information we can obtain on this subject, we can see no parallel in the two cases. Grouchy made an eccentric movement from interior lines, thus changing his interior to an exterior position, leaving the great body of Blucher's army nearer to that of Wellington than he was to Napoleon. Nevertheless, he was near enough to hear the cannonading of Waterloo, and might have reached the field of battle in time to prevent the disastrous retreat, if not to save the defeat. The country was an open one, and his army could have moved as rapidly as that of the enemy. On the contrary, Patterson's position was, from the beginning, an exterior one; he was some sixty miles from the battle-field, with a strong force between him and McDowell. Moreover, Johnston had a railroad at his command, and could reach Manassas Junction in a few hours; whereas, Patterson, without cars (the railroad being obstructed and the bridges destroyed), could not have reached Bull Run in less than two days, to say nothing of the opposition which he would have encountered from the army of Johnston.

"We know nothing of the reasons why Patterson's army was at Martinsburg and Harper's Ferry,—whether his line of operations and his positions were of his own selection, or were the result of superior orders; our criticism is based solely upon the movements as they occurred, without any intention to blame or to exculpate any one."

I now return to my correspondence with the General-in-chief. On the 23d of June, I reported as follows:

"HEADQUARTERS DEPARTMENT OF PENNSYLVANIA,
HAGERSTOWN, MARYLAND, June 23, 1861.

"COLONEL:

"Up to the present instant I have received from Captain J. Newton, Engineer Corps, only a report of a part of his reconnoissance of the Maryland Heights and the ground adjacent, made in compliance with the injunctions of the General-in-chief. I hasten to give the result thus far, expecting to-morrow evening to present the whole.

"Captain Newton approached the Heights from this side, ascending over rough and steep roads, difficult for artillery. The summit he found capable of defence, of ample character, by about 500 men. The main difficulty to be overcome is the supply of water, the springs, which a week since afforded an ample supply, having become dry. He found no water within a half mile of the position selected on the Heights for an intrenched camp. In Pleasant Valley, on the east, near the base of the mountain, springs are reported to abound; their character will be ascertained to-morrow. Water would have to be hauled from this valley, and he reports the ascent very difficult.

"In this valley I propose to place the force sustaining that on the Heights. The whole command, if the location prove favorable, need not exceed 2500 men. That force would render the position safe; anything less would invite attack. The following is what I have to report in relation to the enemy. Deserters from their ranks, some one or more of whom come in daily, all agree in saying that the whole of the force originally at Harper's Ferry (said to have been 25,000 men) is still between Williamsport and Winchester; about 8000 coming this way arrived on Friday at Martinsburg. The remainder are distributed in a semicircle, and on the route to Winchester within four hours' march of the advance. The advance is approaching Falling Waters, under the command of General Jackson, who now commands the whole.

"The force under Jackson controls the people of Berkeley County, who, I believe, are sorely oppressed, and would welcome our approach. That force has become some little encouraged from our not advancing, and may soon annoy us. If so, I shall not avoid the contest they may invite; indeed, if it meets the approval of the General-in-chief, I would march my whole force, as soon as the batteries receive harness, upon the enemy, and drive him step by step to Winchester.

"I believe this force can in ten days rid the adjoining portion of Virginia of its oppressors. I may be forced to this course. My fear is that I may interfere with the general plan of the General-in-chief, and drive the enemy to the aid of the main body.

"They would, however, go as fugitives, to aid in its demoralization. My means of transportation are coming in rapidly.

"I am, sir, very respectfully, your obedient servant,

"R. PATTERSON,
"Major-General, Commanding.

"COLONEL E. D. TOWNSEND,
"A. A. Gen. U. S. Army, Washington City."

I here distinctly state all that I could effect " to drive the enemy to Winchester." Once there I had no doubt that he could intrench and defy me, or by striking the railroad, elude me, and by destroying it or removing the cars, prevent me from following him.

Two days afterwards I received the following (No. 18, p. 125, *Conduct of the War*):

> "HEADQUARTERS OF THE ARMY,
> WASHINGTON, June 25, 1861.
>
> "I write by mail in substance. Remain in front of the enemy while he continues in force between Winchester and the Potomac. If you are in superior or equal force you may cross and attack him. If the enemy should retire upon his resources at Winchester, it is not enjoined that you should pursue him to that distance from your base of operations, without a well-grounded confidence in your continued superiority.
>
> "Your attention is invited to a secondary object, a combined operation on Leesburg between a portion of your troops and the column of Colonel Stone at, and probably above, the Point of Rocks, to hold that village. The enemy has reinforced Leesburg to sixteen hundred (1600) men, and may increase the number. Inquire.
>
> "WINFIELD SCOTT.
>
> "MAJOR-GENERAL PATTERSON."

This gave me the permission I desired, "if I considered myself superior or equal in force to the enemy." I had at this time ten thousand volunteer infantry, six hundred and fifty cavalry and artillery, and six guns, but no means of moving them. The force of the enemy was reported by Captain (now Major-General) Newton, of the U. S. Engineers, who had been for two days engaged at Harper's Ferry in obtaining intelligence, as consisting of fifteen thousand men, and twenty to twenty-four guns; while General Cadwalader's information was that the enemy had twenty guns; "they were counted as they passed." The accuracy of these reports is fully confirmed by the report of General Joseph E. Johnston, which has since been published. He says:

"I assumed command of Harper's Ferry on the 23d of May. The force at that point consisted of nine regiments and two battalions of infantry, four companies of artillery, with sixteen pieces, without caissons, harness, or horses, and about three hundred cavalry. I was employed until the 13th of June in continuing what had been begun by my predecessor, Colonel (now Major-General) Jackson, the organization, instruction, and equipment of the troops, and providing means of transportation and artillery horses. On the morning of the 15th, the army left Harper's Ferry for Winchester. The force had been increased by three regiments (*i. e.*, the Tenth and Thirteenth Virginia and Third Tennessee) since the 1st of June, and encamped four miles beyond Charlestown."

By the admission of the enemy, therefore, his force consisted of 12 regiments and 2 battalions of infantry, 4 companies of artillery, 16 guns, 300 cavalry, which was increased before the 2d of July, when I crossed the river, according to General Johnston, "by the arrival of General Bee and Colonel Elzey, and the Ninth Georgia regiment."

Yet the Commander-in-chief, who had on the 25th given me permission to offer battle "if superior or equal in force," on the 27th, when he knew I had but six guns and no mode of moving them, telegraphs: "I had expected your crossing the river to-day in pursuit of the enemy." To this I wrote the following reply (*Conduct of the War*, p. 126, No. 21):

"HEADQUARTERS DEPARTMENT OF PENNSYLVANIA,
HAGERSTOWN, MARYLAND, June 28, 1861.
" COLONEL :

"I have the honor to acknowledge the receipt of a telegram from the General-in-chief, dated 27th instant, saying: 'I had expected your crossing the river to-day in pursuit of the enemy.'

"I infer from this that orders have been sent me to cross and attack the enemy. If so, I have not received them. Captain Newton, of the Engineers, returned at midnight, after two days' absence in the direction of Sharpsburg and Dam No. 4, and reports, on information he considers reliable, five thousand men from Falling Waters to Dam No. 4, four thousand five hundred men in the vicinity of Shepherdstown under General Jackson, and a reserve of five thousand five hundred men under General Johnston, near Bunker Hill. He also reports twenty to twenty-four guns, and a large cavalry force with General Jackson, and thinks General Negley, whose brigade is on my left, near Sharpsburg, will be attacked, the river being fordable at almost every point. To meet this force of fifteen thousand men, with twenty-two guns, and nearly one thousand cavalry, I have about ten thousand volunteer infantry, and six hundred and fifty cavalry and artillery, the latter being nearly all recruits. The horses are untrained, and we are still without harness for the battery. I have repeatedly asked for batteries, and ought to have one for each brigade, but have none. The only one fit for service sent me was the Rhode Island battery, and that the General-in-chief was compelled, by the necessities of his own position, to take from me, when most wanted, and within a week after it joined me.

"I have neither cavalry nor artillery sufficient to defend the fords of the river between Harper's Ferry and Hancock, but I would much rather attack than defend, and would have more confidence in the result. While I will not, on my own responsibility, attack without artillery and superior force, I will do so cheerfully and promptly if the General-in-chief will give me an explicit order to that effect.

"To insure success, I respectfully but earnestly request that the troops taken from me when Washington was menaced be sent to me with all speed, with a number of field guns equal to those of the insurgents. I will then be enabled to choose my point of attack, offer battle to the enemy, and, I trust, drive them before me, clearing the Valley in front, and taking such position as the General-in-chief may indicate.

"I respectfully suggest that Colonel Stone's column be sent me, with other reinforcements, and venture to add that the sooner I am reinforced with reliable troops and abundant field artillery the better. I am making arrangements for crossing the river, and will do so without waiting for orders or reinforcements, if I find that the strength of the enemy has been overrated.

"I beg to remind the General-in-chief that the period of service of nearly all the troops here will expire within a month, and that, if we do not meet the enemy with them, we will be in no condition to do so for three months to come. The new regiments will not be fit for service before September, if then, and meanwhile this whole frontier will be exposed.

"I have got my command into as good condition as I could expect in so short a time.

"Officers and men are anxious to be led against the insurgents, and if the General-in-chief will give me a regiment of regulars and an adequate force of field artillery, I will cross the river and attack the enemy, unless their forces are ascertained to be more than two to one.

"I beg you to assure the General-in-chief of my sincere desire to sustain him faithfully, and to promote, by all the means at my command, the success of his general plan of operations.

"I am, sir, very respectfully,
   "Your obedient servant,
          "R. PATTERSON,
           "Major-General, Commanding.
"COLONEL E. D. TOWNSEND,
   "Assistant Adjutant-General, U. S. Army,
          "Washington, D. C."

On the 29th of June, the harness for my battery arrived. On the 30th a reconnoissance in force was made, my troops were then concentrated at Williamsport, and on the 2d of July I crossed the Potomac with less than 11,000 men and with one battery of six smooth-bore guns, to which the horses had never been attached until I moved, and to the sound of which they were entirely unaccustomed.

After crossing the Potomac, just beyond Falling Waters, the advance brigade of the enemy, 3500 infantry, with artillery and a large cavalry force, all under "Stonewall" Jackson, were encountered, and after a sharp contest, principally with General Abercrombie's brigade, were forced back and driven before our troops several miles, the relative loss of the enemy being very heavy.

The following official report of the affair was transmitted to the War Department:

"HEADQUARTERS DEPARTMENT OF PENNSYLVANIA,
MARTINSBURG, VIRGINIA, July 6, 1861.

"SIR:

"I telegraphed my intention to cross the Potomac on the 1st instant. I now have the honor to report my movements since that date.

"I left Hagerstown on the afternoon of the 30th ult., the earliest day my command could take the field in a proper condition for active service, intending the following morning to enter Virginia with two columns (at Dam No. 4, and at Williamsport), to be united the same day at Hainesville, the location of the rebels. Owing to the danger and difficulty attending the fording at Dam No. 4, I placed all the force at Williamsport.

"My order of march for the 2d instant is given in the accompanying circular. The advance crossed the Potomac at 4 A. M., all taking the main road to Martinsburg, with the exception of Negley's brigade, which, about one mile from the ford, diverged to the right, to meet the enemy should he come from Hedgesville, to guard our right, and to rejoin at Hainesville.

"About five miles from the ford the skirmishers in front and on the flank suddenly became engaged with the enemy posted in a clump of trees. At the same time their main body appeared in front, sheltered by fences, timber, and houses. Abercrombie immediately deployed his regiments (First Wisconsin and Eleventh Pennsylvania) on each side of the road, placed Hudson's section, supported by the First Troop Philadelphia City Cavalry, in the road, and advanced to the attack against a warm fire before him.

"The enemy being supported by artillery, resisted for twenty-five minutes with much determination. Lieutenant Hudson, after getting in position, soon silenced their guns.

"In the meantime, Thomas's brigade rapidly advanced and deployed to the left flank of the enemy. The enemy, seeing the movement and being pressed by Abercrombie, retired, hotly pursued for four miles by artillery and infantry.

"The cavalry could not be employed, on account of numerous fences and walls crossing the country.

"In the enemy's camp was found camp equipage, provisions, grain, &c.

"This brush was highly creditable to our arms, winning, as we did, the day against a foe superior in numbers to those engaged on our side.

"They were well posted, sheltered by timber, and sustained by artillery and cavalry. Our men advanced over open ground against a warm fire of artillery and infantry. I present the report of Colonels Abercrombie and Thomas, and Lieutenants Perkins and Hudson, and take much pleasure in bearing testimony as an eye-witness to the admirable manner in which their commands were handled, and their commendations earned.

"I also bear testimony to the efficient service, in posting portions of the troops and conducting them to the front and into action, rendered by the members of my staff present and on the field of battle, Colonel Porter, Captain John Newton, and Lieutenant Babcock, and Majors R. Butler Price and Craig Biddle, who were employed conveying orders, also Surgeon Tripler in attending to the wounded.

"The loss of the enemy was over sixty in killed. The number of wounded cannot be ascertained, as a large number were carried off the field.

"I am, sir, very respectfully,
"Your obedient servant,
"R. PATTERSON,
"Major-General, Commanding.
"COLONEL E. D. TOWNSEND,
"Assistant Adjutant-General, U. S. Army,
"Washington, D. C."

Subsequent operations of our forces, upon much grander scales, have caused this brilliant little affair to be forgotten. At the time, however, being the first instance that any number of our troops had been under fire, their gallant behavior in resisting an attack led by so able a commander as "Stonewall" Jackson, was a matter of very general congratulation and natural pride.

On the 3d of July, the army under my command entered Martinsburg. There I was compelled to halt and send back for supplies, and to wait for Colonel Stone's command, ordered on the 30th of June to join me, which he did on the 8th of July. My means of transportation were utterly inadequate, without an increase of which it was impossible to advance. I had wagons and teams for baggage only, and none for a supply train. The reinforcements being without wagons only added to my difficulty. Not one wagon, horse, mule, or set of harness, was sent to me from Washington. All the transportation I had was furnished, under my own orders, by the energetic efforts of my efficient Deputy Quartermaster-General, Colonel Crosman.

As an evidence of this, I insert the following, from other orders of the same character issued at this time (*Report Conduct of the War*, vol. ii, p. 135):

"HEADQUARTERS DEPARTMENT OF PENNSYLVANIA,
MARTINSBURG, July 8, 1861.
"SPECIAL ORDERS, No. 94.

"Division and brigade commanders will require those regiments which have not reduced their number of tents to four common and one wall tent for each company, and one wall tent for other officers, at once to pack the surplus, mark them, and turn them in to Captain Woods, Acting Assistant Quartermaster, at the depot. The spare wagons which will thus be created must be used to carry provisions.

"Every wagon which can be spared from transporting the regiments will at once be taken to Colonel Crosman, who is authorized to call for what he requires.

"The commanding General calls upon every one to reduce their amount of transportation, to enable him to move a larger force to the front, and to keep his army provisioned.

"By order of Major-General Patterson.
"F. J. PORTER,
"Ass't Adjutant-General."

This deficiency of transportation, which I had anticipated on advancing on this line, now began to be a source of serious embarrassment.

Immediately on the arrival of Colonel Stone I issued the following order to advance, the object being to attack the enemy at Winchester (*Report*, vol. ii, p. 135):

"HEADQUARTERS DEPARTMENT OF PENNSYLVANIA,
MARTINSBURG, VA., July 8, 1861.

"GENERAL ORDER. CIRCULAR.

"The troops will move to-morrow morning, in the following order:

"The First (Thomas's) Brigade, with the Rhode Island Battery temporarily attached thereto, will advance by the Winchester turnpike, accompanied by one squadron of cavalry.

"The Seventh (Stone's) Brigade, with Perkins's Battery attached thereto, will take the main street of the town (by the Court-house), and will continue on the road parallel to and east of the Winchester turnpike. One company of cavalry will be attached to this command.

"The First (Cadwalader's) Division will follow the march of Thomas's Brigade. Doubleday's Battery will advance with this division, one regiment of which will be detailed for its guard, to accompany wherever it may be ordered.

"The Second (Keim's) Division will pursue both routes, General Negley's Brigade following the march of Colonel Stone and Colonel Abercrombie's, and General Wynkoop's that of General Cadwalader.

"The Twenty-eighth and Nineteenth New York Regiments will be temporarily attached to General Keim's Division.

"General Keim will detail a strong rear-guard of his division for the wagon train. The rear-guard will march on the flanks and rear of the train, and will be reinforced by a squadron of cavalry.

"General Keim will detail a competent field-officer to command the rear-guard.

"The wagons will advance in one train in the rear of the troops, and will be required to keep closed.

"The troops of the several divisions and brigades will keep closed.

"By order of Major-General Patterson.
"F. J. PORTER,
"Ass't Adjutant-General."

About midnight the order was countermanded, as some of the troops that had arrived under Colonel Stone were reported by him so weary and footsore as to be quite unable, without repose, to bear the fatigue of a further march, and be in a condition to fight.

On the next morning, the 9th of July, finding from conversation with some of my officers that their opposition to the plan of advancing upon Winchester, made known by the circular, appeared to be very strong and decided, I was induced, before renewing the order, to call a council of all the division and brigade commanders, the officers of Engineers, and chiefs of the Departments of Transportation and Supply. These were: Major-General Wm. H. Keim, Brigadier-General Cadwalader (now Major-General), Colonel Abercrombie (now Brigadier-General), Colonel Geo. H. Thomas (now Major-General), Brigadier-General Negley (now Major-General), Colonel Stone (now Brigadier-General), Captain Newton, U. S. Engineers (now Major-General), Captain Simpson, U. S. Topographical Engineers (now Colonel), Captain Beckwith, Subsistence Department (now Colonel), Lieutenant-Colonel Crosman, Quartermaster's Department (now Colonel): seven distinguished officers of the regular service, and three experienced officers of the Volunteers, the survivors of whom are all now in the service, where they have earned new laurels and high promotion.

I had the less hesitation in consulting with these officers, because, after they were ordered to my command, and I was about to attack Harper's Ferry, the

General-in-chief, in his despatch of June 8th, already quoted, says:

"I have said that we must sustain no reverse; but this is not enough: a check or a drawn battle would be a victory to the enemy, filling his heart with joy, his ranks with men, and his magazines with voluntary contributions.

"Take your measures, therefore, circumspectly; make good use of your engineers and other experienced staff officers and generals, and attempt nothing without a clear prospect of success, as you will find the enemy strongly posted and not inferior to you in numbers."

The suggestion of a council coming from these very "engineers, staff officers, and generals," I felt bound not to disregard, and, in case of disaster, I could scarcely say that "I had attempted nothing without a clear prospect of success," if my defeat had been foretold by the very men I was expected to consult. I submitted to the council my instructions, orders, and the following statement (*Report Conduct of the War*, vol. ii, pp. 85, 86, 87):

"This force was collected originally to retake Harper's Ferry. That evacuated, it was directed to remain as long as Johnston remained in force in this vicinity. Threatening, as he was, either to move to the aid of the force attacking Washington, or annoying the frontier of Maryland, this army was permitted to cross the Potomac and offer battle.
"If accepted, so soon as Johnston was defeated, to return and approach Washington.
"The enemy retires, for what? Is it weakness, or a trap? Can we continue to advance, and pursue if he retires? If so, how far? When shall we retire?

"Our volunteer force will soon dwindle before us, and we may be left without aid. If our men go home without a regular battle, a good field fight, they will go home discontented, will not re-enlist, and will sour the minds of others. We have a long line to defend, liable at any moment to be cut off from our base and depot, and to a blow on our flank.

"Our forces must not be defeated, nor checked in battle, or meet with reverses. It would be fatal to our cause.

"A force threatens Washington. If we abandon our present position, Johnston will be available to aid.

"The command has been largely reinforced to enable us to sustain our position, to clear the valley to Winchester, to defeat the enemy if he accepts battle, and to be in position to aid General McDowell, or to move upon Washington, Richmond, or elsewhere, as the General-in-chief may direct. General Sanford, with two rifled guns and three regiments, will be up to-morrow.

"Our force will then be as large as it ever will be. Under the prospect of losing a large portion of our force in a few days, by expiration of service, what shall be done?"

The result of the deliberation is given in the following minute, taken at the time by Major Craig Biddle, of the staff (*Report*, vol. ii, p. 85, &c.):

"*Minutes of Council of War, held July 9, 1861, at Martinsburg, Virginia.*

"Colonel Crosman, Quartermaster, thought nine hundred wagons would be sufficient to furnish subsistence, and to transport ammunition to our present force. The calculation for the original column was seven hundred wagons, of which five hundred were on hand and two hundred expected. The great difficulty will be to obtain forage for the animals, the present consumption being twenty-six tons daily.

"Captain Beckwith, Commissary. The question of subsistence is here a question of transportation. Thus far no reliance has been placed on the adjacent country. A day's march ahead would compel a resort to it. As far as known those supplies would be quite inadequate.

"Captain Simpson, Topographical Engineers. The difficulty of our present position arises from the great facility the enemy has to concentrate troops at Winchester from Manassas Junction. By the railroad, twelve thousand men could be sent there in a day, and again sent back to Manassas. Our forces should combine with the forces at Washington.

"Captain Newton, Engineers. Our present position is a very exposed one. General Johnston can keep us where we are as long as he pleases, and at any time make a demonstration on our rear. Our whole line is a false one. We have no business here, except for the purpose of making a demonstration. He threatens *us* now. We should be in a position to threaten him. We should go to Charlestown, Harper's Ferry, Shepherdstown, and flank him.

"Colonel Stone. It is mainly a question for the staff. Our enemy has great facility of movement, and to extend our line would be accompanied with great danger. Johnston should be threatened from some other point. We might leave two regiments here, two guns at Shepherdstown, and proceed to Charlestown, and threaten from that point.

"General Negley, ditto to Captain Newton.

"Colonel Thomas approves of a flank movement to Charlestown.

"Colonel Abercrombie, the same.

"General Keim, the same.

"General Cadwalader opposed to a forward movement."

The wisdom of this decision of the council held on the 9th was confirmed in my mind by the receipt of the following telegram from the General-in-chief two days afterwards (see *Conduct of the War*, vol. ii, p. 86):

"WAR DEPARTMENT,
WASHINGTON, July 11, 1861.

"MAJOR-GENERAL PATTERSON,
"Martinsburg, Virginia.

"The author of the following is known, and he believes it authentic:

"'WASHINGTON, July 9, 1861.

"'The plan of operations of the Secession army in Virginia contemplates the reverse of the proceedings and movements announced in the Express of yesterday and Saturday. A schedule that has come to light meditates a stand and an engagement by Johnston, when he shall have drawn Patterson sufficiently far back from the river to render impossible his retreat across it on being vanquished, and an advance then by Johnston and Wise conjointly upon McClellan, and, after the conquest of him, a march in this direction, to unite in an attack upon the Federal forces across the Potomac, with the army under Beauregard at Manassas Junction, and the wing of that army, the South Carolina regiments chiefly, now nine (9) miles from Alexandria. Success in each of these three several movements is anticipated, and thereby not only the possession of the capital is thought to be assured, but an advance of the Federal troops upon Richmond prevented. The plan supposes that this success will give the Confederate cause such *prestige*, and inspire in it such faith, as will insure the recognition of its Government abroad, and at the same time so impair confidence in the Federal Government as to render it impossible for it to procure loans abroad, and very difficult for it to raise means at home. Real retreats, which have been anticipated, it will be seen are, by this plan, altogether ignored. According to it, fighting and conquest are the orders.'

"E. D. TOWNSEND,
"Asst. Adjt. Genl."

This paper, transmitted from the headquarters of the army, speaks for itself.

That this was the plan agreed upon by the Confederate generals there is no doubt; and it was a judicious one. My information of a similar kind had come from various quarters. My most experienced officers of the regular service, with whom I fully and freely consulted, Colonels George H. Thomas, Abercrombie, and Crosman, Major Fitz John Porter, Captains Newton, Beckwith, and many others, men of long service, merit, and great experience, all concurred in the opinion that I was too far advanced at Martinsburg; that Johnston had fallen back for no other purpose than to lead me on; that he had a trap set somewhere, and that, if not very cautious, I should fall into it.

Each of these officers, not only approved warmly of the management of my command, but opposed, both in and out of council, a further advance. With their opposition to an advance well known, five of the number have since been made general officers.

The enemy were at Winchester intrenched. The phrase "intrenchments," at the beginning of the war, was very much misunderstood, and was popularly supposed to refer to permanent works. Experience has shown, on several occasions, that earthworks thrown up in a night have defied the efforts of the best troops.

The superiority of the enemy at Winchester in men and guns as well as in position, was well known. The information was obtained from Union men who had been there, from prisoners, from deserters, and from other sources, all agreeing on an average of about forty thousand men and over sixty guns. Captain Wellmore, belonging to a Maryland regiment, taken prisoner at Charlestown by a party sent by me from Harper's Ferry, gave forty thousand. A gentleman from Berkeley County, of high respectability, serving under Johnston as an unwilling Virginia volunteer in Jackson's Brigade, at the battle of Falling Waters, subsequently gave the following statement, taken down by General Negley, and by him given to me:

"General Jackson retreated with his brigade, consisting then of four regiments and four pieces of artillery (Captain Pendleton), to Big Spring, three and a half miles south of Martinsburg. General Johnston arrived at Darkesville the same night with about fourteen thousand men. He was then reinforced by one regiment and one battery (four guns) flying artillery. General Jackson retreated to that point. The army made a stand there for four days; they then retreated to Winchester. When we arrived there, we found fortifications commenced by the militia. All the army there assisted, and in two days the city was fortified all around, within two miles of the suburbs, with intrenchments. Reinforcements commenced pouring in. Ten 42-pounders were placed, masked, around the fortifications; also, artificial thickets planted for riflemen. The force consisted of forty-two thousand, including four thousand militia. General Johnston then received a despatch, as read to the men, that General Patterson was out of the way; that he had gone to get in Beauregard's rear, and that Jeff. Davis had ordered him to cut off General Patterson, in order to save the country; that General Beauregard had been attacked by an overwhelming force. General Johnston's army moved at 1 o'clock, P.M., Thursday, consisting of nine brigades, with fifty-two pieces of flying artillery, including three ten-inch columbiads, represented to me as such. Among the artillery was a detachment of the Washington Artillery, consisting of eight guns, four of which were rifled cannon. General Johnston took with him thirty-five thousand men, leaving the militia and volunteers, to the number of seven thousand, in Winchester."

Mr. McDonald, a reporter, gave the following statement, taken down by General Cadwalader, and by him given to me:

" General Johnston's force at Winchester was forty-two thousand men, infantry, artillery, and cavalry; of which, eight hundred were Virginia cavalry, under Colonel Stuart, and three hundred from Southern States. Forty regiments, thirty-five thousand men, left Winchester, at 1 o'clock P. M., on Thursday, by order of General Beauregard; took the road to Berry's Ford, on the Shenandoah, thirteen and a half miles, over the Blue Ridge to Piedmont Station, on the Manassas Gap Railroad, fifteen miles, making twenty-eight and a half miles, requiring two days' march. Freight and passenger cars had been hauled over the road, on their own wheels, to Strasburg last week, and on them Johnston's forces were expected to be transported, on the Manassas Railroad, from Piedmont to Manassas Junction, thirty-eight to forty miles. There remained at Winchester seven thousand troops until Saturday afternoon, when they left for Strasburg, on their way to Manassas, except about two thousand five hundred of the militia of the neighboring counties, disbanded and sent home. A large quantity of arms in boxes was sent to Strasburg. The Virginia cavalry remained (under Colonel Stuart), and went to Berrysville to observe the movements of General Patterson's column. The rest of the cavalry went with General Johnston. They had at Winchester sixty-two pieces of artillery in position in the fortifications; about ten 42-pounders (some, they thought, were columbiads) were left. The remainder were taken by General Johnston. A detachment of the Washington Artillery, from New Orleans, had eight heavy guns, of which four were 32-pounders. These were hauled by twenty-eight horses each; the rest (smaller guns) by six and four horses each. Part, if not all of them, were brass rifled guns. The fortifications surrounded Winchester, except to the southward, upon the high ground; very heavy earthworks, made with bags and barrels filled with earth, &c. In front of the breastworks deep trenches were dug, communicating below with inside of the works. The guns were all masked with artificial thickets of evergreens, which were intended in some cases to be used as ambuscades for riflemen and sharpshooters. Among the regiments was one of Kentucky riflemen, armed with heavy bowie-knives. They refused to take more than one round of cartridges. They proposed to place themselves in the bushes for assault. All the fences had been levelled for miles in front of Winchester. The fortifications extended two and a half miles. The trees had been felled between Bunker Hill and Winchester, to impede an advance. Fifteen hundred sick at Winchester, confined with measles, dysentery, and typhoid fever. Prisoners taken from our column were sent to Richmond. Wise had been recalled, it is said, with his troops, from Western Virginia. Beauregard and Davis had done it in opposition to General Lee's advice."

Mr. Lackland, brother of Colonel Lackland, residing a short distance from Charlestown, and just returned from Winchester, stated, July 20th, 1861, that Johnston had at that place,

"2 regiments from Kentucky, Duncan and Pope,	1,800
2 regiments from Tennessee,	1,800
5 regiments from Alabama, strong,	4,500
5 regiments from Georgia, strong,	4,600
1 regiment from North Carolina,	1,000
5 regiments from Mississippi,	4,500
2 regiments from Maryland,	1,200
Several regiments from Virginia,	10,000
Militia from Virginia,	5,000
One regiment of cavalry,	600
Several batteries,	700
	35,200

"On Wednesday, the 18th, at 2 P.M., he commenced his movement southeast. Number taken, 30,000 Confederate troops; number left, 5200 militia."

These statements, with many others, taken by different officers, from different persons, at different times and places, agree very much in the main facts.

Like most other reports, these were doubtless exaggerated, and required, as they received, due allowance. We are not, however, to rush into the other extreme, and believe nothing, because the narrator may be supposed to have exceeded the truth. We have in the present case a most valuable witness, one whose interest it was to underrate his own force and overrate mine, General Johnston himself. Stating my force at thirty thousand, he alleges his inferiority in men as a reason for not attacking me, and would therefore, to justify himself, make his force as small as possible. By his official report he had, on the 23d of May, 9 regiments and 2 battalions of infantry, 4 companies of artillery, 16 pieces of artillery, 300 cavalry. To this were added, on the 13th of June, 3 regiments of infantry, and, on the 15th of July, 8 regiments of infantry, with 2500 militia to man the fortifications. Of intrenchments he says that, after my first advance across the Potomac, on the 16th of June, "Major Whiting was ordered to plan defensive works, and to have some heavy guns on navy carriages mounted. About twenty-five hundred militia, under Brigadier-General Carson, were called out to man them."

General Scott, also, in a despatch addressed to my successor, General Banks, which I received before I was relieved, gives the following information as to the number of guns which Johnston had *left behind him* at Winchester (*Report*, vol. ii, p. 140):

"War Department,
Washington, July 23, 11.30 p.m.

"The following information has just been received from A. N. Rankin, editor of the Republican and Transcript: There are nine 32-pounders, four 44-pounders, and two 6-pounders, and one thousand stand of arms at Winchester, with but five hundred men, raw militia, to guard the same. There are also one thousand tents, and a very large amount of powder, balls, and shells.

"Winfield Scott.

"Major-General Banks,
"Headquarters Army, Harper's Ferry."

General Abercrombie, a regular officer of more than forty years' service, writes me from Winchester on the 17th of March, 1862:

"I rode over the ground occupied by Johnston in July, and, after a careful examination, I found that I had no reason to change my opinion as to the course you adopted.

"The works themselves were of no great strength, but the judicious disposition made of them, the favorable character of the ground, size and number of guns, and numerical strength of force, ought to have defeated double the number.

"I think you may rely on this: Johnston had twenty-six thousand volunteers that were mustered into the service, and between six and seven thousand of what they call militia, making some thirty-two or thirty-three thousand men. The trenches extend some four or five miles. They commence at the turnpike leading to Charlestown, due east from Winchester, and run to the base of the hills west of the town, and at every few hundred paces we found platforms for heavy pivot guns, some of them rifled, so I am told. On the hills alluded to, some very heavy guns were admirably arranged, and commanded the whole valley. These also were made to traverse in every direction. Most of these earthworks were constructed with regard to the Martinsburg route. On the 16th, Johnston had his whole force under arms, in battle order, and waited some hours, under the impression that you were approaching from Bunker Hill to attack him, and has since said he regrets not having attacked you.

"General Johnston had not *less* than thirty-two thousand men, a very strong position, and between sixty and seventy guns, eleven of them pivot and of heavy calibre.

"I have conversed with a number of intelligent persons on the subject, and all agree very nearly as to the strength of Johnston's force and number of guns, and my own observations and personal inspection (of the abandoned earthworks) satisfy me of the correctness of their statements."

I will here take occasion to say that my force was always greatly overestimated, not only by the public, but apparently by the General-in-chief himself. There were twelve regiments ordered to join me, one Delaware and three New Jersey on the 24th of May, two New York on the 30th of May, two Ohio and two Northern regiments on the 4th of June, and two Pennsylvania on the 10th of June, but they never did so. I was, therefore, probably operating with a force less by twelve regiments than the General-in-chief intended : a fact sufficient to explain his exaggerated ideas of the strength of my command. My largest force was accumulated at Martinsburg, about eighteen thousand two hundred men. When I marched from there, I had to leave two regiments, taking about sixteen thousand eight hundred men with me, and, deducting from them the sick, the rear and wagon guards, I could not have gone into action with more than thirteen thousand, and at the time Johnston marched from Winchester I could not have taken into action ten thousand men.

If I had been defeated a large portion of my army would have probably been destroyed and the others made prisoners of war. The affair would have been more disastrous than Bull Run, for the Potomac was behind me and I had no reserves to fall back upon. The enemy, flushed with two victories instead of one, with no army in position to check them, might have been in possession of Washington, Baltimore, and Philadelphia, within five days. The reason assigned for not advancing on Washington by the commander of the Confederates in his official report after Bull Run, was the fact of my army being intact and ready to advance. This Shenandoah Valley, through which the enemy have since twice penetrated into Pennsylvania, I was always loath to leave unguarded. On the 20th of June, when about to cross the Potomac, I had written to General McCall as follows: (*Report*, vol. ii, p. 82):

"HEADQUARTERS, DEPARTMENT OF PENNSYLVANIA,
HAGERSTOWN, June 26, 1861.

"MY DEAR GENERAL:

"If I can get permission to go over into Virginia, I intend to cross the river and offer battle to the insurgents. As the regulars and Rhode Island regiment and battery have been taken from me, I will require all the force now here, and must leave the Pennsylvania line unguarded. Please inform me how many men you can throw forward, and how soon.

"Very respectfully and truly yours,
"R. PATTERSON."

To which Major-General McCall replied as follows (p. 82):

"HARRISBURG, Sunday, June 30, 1861.

"MY DEAR GENERAL:

"On my return from Pittsburg this morning, I find your note of the 26th instant, informing me of your purpose to cross the river and offer battle to the insurgents, and asking what force I can throw forward on the Pennsylvania line.

"In reply I have to say that the only force (one regiment rifles, and one infantry, with a section of artillery) of my command as yet armed and equipped, has been pushed forward to the support of Colonel Wallace at Cumberland, and for the protection of our border settlers in that direction; the other regiments are without clothing, arms, or equipments, still, notwithstanding my efforts to fit them for the field. You will therefore perceive how impossible it will be for me, although I much regret it, to comply with your request.

"With great regard, very truly yours,
"GEORGE A. McCALL."

It will be seen from the letter of General McCall that with all his efforts, he had but two regiments and a section of artillery fit for the field, and this force, under Colonel Charles J. Biddle, was then beyond Bedford, "for the support of Colonel Wallace at Cumberland, and for the protection of our border settlers in that direction." I was thus made responsible for our entire frontier from Cumberland to Edwards' Ferry, while I had not cavalry or artillery enough to guard the fords between Hancock and Harper's Ferry. These were some of the reasons which prevented me from attacking the enemy at Winchester. My instructions were, "If the enemy were to retire upon his resources at Winchester, it is not enjoined that you pursue him to that distance from your base of operations without a *well-grounded confidence in your continued superiority.*"

Will any fair-minded man say, that I could under these circumstances have entertained any such confidence?

But what was to be gained by an attack, the object being to detain Johnston?

I had been anxious to go to Leesburg, where, if Johnston attempted to elude me, I could reach McDowell as soon as he could join Beauregard. This, however, was not permitted, but I was kept on a false line, where I could no more prevent Johnston by force from going to Manassas than an army at Washington could prevent one at Philadelphia going to New York. Neither could I follow him, for he had a railroad behind him which he could use and then destroy. Johnston says, in his official report, "I proceeded to Winchester. There the army was in position to oppose either McClellan from the west, or Patterson from the northeast, and to form a junction with General Beauregard when necessary."

After the conference with my officers, I wrote to the General-in-chief, as follows:

"HEADQUARTERS DEPARTMENT OF PENNSYLVANIA,
MARTINSBURG, July 9, 1861.

"COLONEL:

"I have received the telegrams of the General-in-chief, notifying of the additional regiments sent to me. Colonel Stone and the Nineteenth and Twenty-eighth New York regiments arrived yesterday. General Sanford, with the Fifth and Twelfth New York regiments, will join to-morrow.

"Since I last addressed you, I have made no movements;

in fact, have been prevented by the necessity of sending all my wagons to the rear, to obtain provisions for a few days in advance and to bring up troops. The commissary has supplies (with those in hands of troops) for about two days. Though the quartermaster has spared no exertion, and his agents have been very active, he has not as yet been able to provide a supply train for the command. I am, therefore, much restricted in my movements, being compelled after three days' advance to send back for provisions. The difficulty will increase as I advance; indeed, I am now almost at a stand. Instead of receiving aid from the inhabitants, I find myself in an enemy's country, where our opponents can procure supplies and we nothing, except by seizure. Even information is studiously kept from us. Supplies, especially provisions, are very scarce, and not even one day's rations can be relied upon. The supply of grain also is very limited. Under these circumstances, I respectfully present to the General-in-chief the following plan, which with my present views I desire to carry into operation so soon as I can do so with safety, and the necessity for following Johnston ceases. I propose to move this force to Charlestown, from which point I can more easily strike Winchester, march to Leesburg when necessary, open communication to a depot to be established at Harper's Ferry, and occupy the main avenue of supply to the enemy. My base will then be some seven miles nearer, more easily reached by road, and my line of communication rendered more secure than at present. I can establish communication with the Maryland shore by a bridge of boats. In this way I can more easily approach you, and the movement, I think, will tend to relieve Leesburg and vicinity of some of its oppressors. My present location is a very bad one, in a military point of view, and from it I cannot move a portion of the force without exposing what remains to be cut off.

"General Sanford informs me by letter that he has for me a letter from you. I hope it will inform me when you will put your column in motion against Manassas, and when you wish me to strike. The enemy retired in succession from

Darkesville and Bunker Hill to Stevenson's Station, a few miles from Winchester. There he has halted, and report says is intrenching. His design evidently is to draw this force on as far as possible from its base, and then to cut my line, or to attack with large reinforcements from Manassas. As I have already stated, I cannot advance far, and if I could, I think the movement very imprudent. When you make your attack I expect to advance and offer battle. If the enemy retires, shall not pursue. I am very desirous to know when the General-in-chief wishes me to approach Winchester. If the notice does not come in any other way, I wish you would indicate the day by telegraph thus: '*Let me hear from you on ——.*'

"I am, sir, very respectfully,
"Your obedient servant,
"R. PATTERSON,
"Major-General, Commanding.
"COLONEL E. D. TOWNSEND,
"Assistant Adjutant-General U. S. Army,
"Washington, D. C."

On the 13th I received the following telegram from General Scott:

"WASHINGTON, July 12, 1861, 1.30 P.M.

"Go where you propose in your letter of the 9th instant. Should that movement cause the enemy to retreat upon Manassas *via* Strasburg, to follow him at this distance would seem hazardous, whereas the route from Charlestown *via* Keyes' Ferry, Hillsboro', and Leesburg, towards Alexandria, with the use of the canal on the other side of the river for transportation, may be practicable. Consider this suggestion well, and, except in extreme case, do not recross the Potomac with more than a sufficient detachment for your supplies on the canal. *Let me hear from you on Tuesday.* Write often when *en route.*

"WINFIELD SCOTT.
"MAJOR-GENERAL PATTERSON,
"Martinsburg, Virginia."

This gave me the desired permission to go to Charlestown; and the phrase, "Let me hear from you on Tuesday," announced that General McDowell's attack was to begin on that day.

On the next day, the orders were substantially reiterated in the following despatch:

"WASHINGTON, July 13, 1861.

"I telegraphed you yesterday, if not strong enough to beat the enemy early next week, make demonstrations so as to detain him in the valley of Winchester; but if he retreats in force towards Manassas, and it be hazardous to follow him, then consider the route *via* Keyes' Ferry, Leesburg, &c.

"WINFIELD SCOTT.

"GENERAL R. PATTERSON."

I did not consider myself "strong enough to beat the enemy," nor did any officer with whom I consulted; I determined, therefore, "to make demonstrations so as to detain Johnston in the valley of Winchester" at the time indicated. This gave me no opportunity to change my base promptly, and the attempt to do so I thought might send Johnston to Manassas at the very time the General-in-chief desired him to be kept at Winchester, to wit, on the following Tuesday. I therefore postponed my movement to Charlestown until after that day. This I considered a fulfilment of my orders to the very letter, and as I reported every movement I was making fully to headquarters, as appears by the following letters, I could at any moment have been stopped by telegraph, had it been desired that I should act differently (*Report*, vol. ii, pp. 132, 138, 139):

"HEADQUARTERS DEPARTMENT OF PENNSYLVANIA,
MARTINSBURG, July 14th, 1861.
"COLONEL E. D. TOWNSEND,
"Assistant Adjutant-General U. S. Army,
"Washington City.

"COLONEL: I have thus far succeeded in keeping in this vicinity the command under General Johnston, who is now pretending to be engaged in fortifying at Winchester, but prepared to retire beyond striking distance if I shall advance far.

"To-morrow I advance to Bunker Hill, preparatory to the other movement. If an opportunity offers I shall attack, but unless I can rout shall be careful not to set him in full retreat upon Strasburg.

"I have arranged for the occupation of Harper's Ferry, opposite which point I have directed provisions to be sent.

"Many of the three months' volunteers are very restless at the prospect of being retained over their time. This fact will cause you to hear from me soon in the direction of Charlestown. Want of ample transportation for supplies and baggage has prevented my moving earlier in the direction I desired.

"I am, sir, very respectfully, your obedient servant,
"R. PATTERSON,
"Major-General, Commanding."

"HEADQUARTERS DEPARTMENT OF PENNSYLVANIA,
BUNKER HILL, July 16th, 1861.
"COLONEL E. D. TOWNSEND,
"Assistant Adjutant-General U. S. Army,
"Washington City.

"COLONEL: I have the honor to report, for the information of the General-in-chief, my advance and arrival at this place yesterday, opposed only by a body of six hundred cavalry, of which one was killed and five taken prisoners.

"To-morrow I move upon Charlestown. A reconnoissance shows the Winchester road blocked by fallen trees and fences placed across it, indicating no confidence in the large force now said to be at Winchester. I send you a sketch, prepared by Captain Simpson, of the works said to have been erected in the vicinity of Winchester.

"Preparations have already been commenced to occupy and hold Harper's Ferry with the three years' troops. If the General-in-chief desires to retain that place (and I advise it never to be evacuated), I desire to be at once informed by telegraph.

"I have to report that the term of service of a very large portion of this force will expire in a few days. From an undercurrent expression of feeling, I am confident that many will be inclined to lay down their arms the day the term expires. With such a feeling existing, any active operations cannot be thought of, until they are replaced by three years' men. Those whose terms expire this week, and will not remain, I shall arrange to send off by Harper's Ferry; those for Philadelphia *via* Baltimore, those for Harrisburg *via* Hagerstown.

"If Harper's Ferry is to be held, after securing that, I shall, if the General-in-chief desires, advance with the remainder of the troops *via* Leesburg, provided the force under Johnston does not remain at Winchester after the success which I anticipate from General McDowell.

"I wish to be advised if these propositions meet with the approval of the General-in-chief.

"The Wisconsin regiments are without arms and accoutrements, which I have directed the commander of the Frankford Arsenal to provide.

"I am, sir, very respectfully, your obedient servant,

"R. PATTERSON,
"Major-General, Commanding."

"HEADQUARTERS DEPARTMENT OF PENNSYLVANIA,
CHARLESTOWN, VIRGINIA, July 17, 1861.

"The terms of service of the Pennsylvania troops (eighteen regiments) expire within seven days, commencing to-morrow. I can rely on none of them renewing service. I must be at once provided with efficient three years' men, or withdraw to Harper's Ferry.

"Shall I occupy permanently Harper's Ferry, or withdraw entirely? I wrote yesterday on this subject, and now wish to be informed of the intentions of the General-in-chief. My march to-day was without opposition or incident of importance. The country has been drained of men. This place has been a depot for supplies for the force at Winchester, and the presence of the army is not welcome.

"R. Patterson,
"Major-General, Commanding.

"Colonel E. D. Townsend,
"Assistant Adjutant-General U. S. Army,
"Washington, D. C."

"Headquarters of the Army,
Washington, July 17, 1861.

"I have nothing official from you since Sunday, but am glad to learn, through Philadelphia papers, that you have advanced. Do not let the enemy amuse and delay you with a small force in front while he reinforces the Junction with his main body.

"McDowell's first day's work has driven the enemy beyond Fairfax Court-house. The Junction will probably be carried to-morrow.

"Winfield Scott.

"General Patterson,
"Commanding U. S. Forces, Harper's Ferry."

To this I replied as follows:

"Headquarters Department of Pennsylvania,
Charlestown, Virginia, July 18, 1861.

"Telegram of to-day received. The enemy has stolen no march upon me. I have kept him actively employed, and by threats and reconnoissance in force, caused him to be reinforced. I have accomplished more in this respect than the General-in-chief asked, or could well be expected in face of an enemy far superior in numbers, with no line of communication to protect.

"In future, Post-office, Sandy Hook.

"R. Patterson,
"Major-General, Commanding.

"Colonel E. D. Townsend,
"Assistant Adjutant-General U. S. Army,
"Washington."

On the same day I received the following:

"HEADQUARTERS OF THE ARMY,
WASHINGTON, July 18, 1861.

"I have certainly been expecting you to beat the enemy; if not, to hear that you had felt him strongly, or at least had occupied him by threats and demonstrations. You have been at least his equal, and I suppose, superior in number. Has he not stolen a march and sent reinforcements toward Manassas Junction? A week is enough to win a victory. The time of volunteers counts from the day mustered into the service of the United States. You must not retreat across the Potomac. If necessary, when abandoned by the short term volunteers, intrench somewhere and wait for reinforcements.

"WINFIELD SCOTT.
"MAJOR-GENERAL PATTERSON,
"Commanding U. S. Forces."

To this I replied:

"HEADQUARTERS DEPARTMENT OF PENNSYLVANIA,
CHARLESTOWN, VIRGINIA,
July 18, 1861, 1.30 A. M.

"Telegram of date received. Mine of to-night gives the condition of my command. Some regiments have given warning not to serve an hour over time. To attack under such circumstances against the greatly superior force at Winchester is most hazardous. My letter of the 16th gives you further information. *Shall I attack?*

"R. PATTERSON,
"Major-General, Commanding.
"COLONEL E. D. TOWNSEND,
"Assistant Adjutant-General U. S. Army,
"Washington, D. C."

(To same, 1 P. M.)

"I have succeeded, in accordance with the wishes of the General-in-chief, in keeping General Johnston's force at Winchester. A reconnoissance in force on Tuesday caused him to be largely reinforced from Strasburg. With the existing feeling and determination of the three months' men to return home, it would be ruinous to advance, or even to stay here without immediate increase of force to replace them. They will not remain.

"I have ordered the brigades to assemble this afternoon, and shall make a formal appeal to the troops to stay a few days until I can be reinforced. Many of the regiments are without shoes; the Government refuses to furnish them; the men have received no pay; and neither officers or soldiers have money to purchase with. Under these circumstances I cannot ask or expect the three months' volunteers to stay longer than one week. Two companies of Pennsylvania volunteers were discharged to-day and ordered home. I to-day place additional force at Harper's Ferry and establish communication with Maryland. I sent Captain Newton to prepare for its defence.

"R. PATTERSON,
"Major-General, Commanding."

· Thus, from Charlestown on Thursday, the 18th of July, three days before the battle of Bull Run, at 1.30 A.M., twelve hours before any part of General Johnston's command left Winchester for Manassas, I telegraphed General Scott my opinion of the probable result of an attack on Winchester, and asked, "Shall I attack?"

To this no answer was returned, and I was left in utter ignorance of General McDowell's movements from Wednesday, July 17th, until Monday, the 22d, when I first heard of the disastrous result through the newspapers. If the Commander-in-chief, who was perfectly acquainted with my condition, desired me to attack, he here had an opportunity of directing it; with his order, I would cheerfully have advanced, let my force have been what it would and the result what it might. And if General Scott had desired me to join him at Manassas, an order to me at that time would have effected it, and I could have been there, if ordered on that day, as soon or sooner than Johnston.

On the same day the following letter was also sent:

"HEADQUARTERS DEPARTMENT OF PENNSYLVANIA,
CHARLESTOWN, VIRGINIA, July 18, 1861.

"COLONEL:

"I arrived at this place on the 17th instant. Nothing of importance occurred on the march. The principal inhabitants left some days since, anticipating its occupation by the Federal troops. It was, till our arrival, the location of a band of Secession militia, engaged in pressing into the service the young men of the country. I have to acknowledge the receipt of two telegrams from the General-in-chief, of the 17th and 18th instant, both looking to a movement and attack upon Winchester. A state of affairs existed which the General-in-chief is not aware of, though in some respects anticipated by his instructions, that if I found the enemy too strong to attack, to threaten and make demonstrations to retain him at Winchester. I more than carried out the wishes of the General-in-chief in this respect. Before I left Martinsburg, I was informed of a large increase in Johnston's command, and of the visit to Winchester of the leading members of the Confederate army. Just before General McDowell was to strike, I advanced to Bunker Hill, causing surprise, and I have since learned an additional increase of force. On Tuesday I sent out a reconnoitring party towards Winchester. It drove the enemy's pickets, and caused the army to be formed in line of battle, anticipating an attack from my main force. This party found the road barricaded and blocked by fallen trees. The following day I left for this place.

"Before marching from Martinsburg, I heard of the mutterings of many of the volunteer regiments, and their expressed determination not to serve one hour after their term of service should expire. I anticipated a better expression of opinion as we approached the enemy, and hoped to hear of a willingness to remain a week or ten days. I was disappointed; and when I prepared for a movement to the front, by an order for the men to carry two days' provisions in their haversacks, I was assailed by earnest remonstrance against being detained over their term of service, complaints from officers of want of shoes and other clothing, all throwing obstacles in the way of active operations. Indeed, I found I should, if I took Winchester, be without men, and be forced to retreat, thus losing the fruits of victory. Under these circumstances, neither I nor those on whom I could rely, could advance with any confidence. I am, therefore, now here, with a force which will be dwindling away very rapidly. I to-day appealed almost in vain to the regiments to stand by the country for a week or ten days. The men are longing for their homes, and nothing can detain them. I sent Captain Newton to-day to Harper's Ferry to arrange for defence and re-establish communication with Maryland, and the Massachusetts regiments. The Third Wisconsin will soon be there. Lieutenant Babcock has been at Sandy Hook several days trying to get the canal in operation, prepare the entrance to the ford, putting in operation a ferry, and reconstructing the bridge. Depots for all supplies will soon be established, and there I shall cause to be turned in the camp equipage, &c., of the regiments, and to that place I shall withdraw if I find my force so small as to render my present position unsafe. I cannot intrench sufficiently to defend this place against a large force.

"I shall direct the regiments to be sent to Harrisburg and Philadelphia, to be mustered out by Captain Hastings, Major Ruff, and Captain Wharton.

"I am, sir, very respectfully, your obedient servant,
 "R. PATTERSON,
 "Major-General, Commanding.
"COLONEL E. D. TOWNSEND,
 "Assistant Adjutant-General U. S. Army,
  "Washington, D. C."

> "HEADQUARTERS DEPARTMENT OF PENNSYLVANIA,
> CHARLESTOWN, VIRGINIA, July 19, 1861.
>
> "Almost all the three months' volunteers refuse to serve an hour over their time, and, except three regiments which will stay ten days, the most of them are without shoes or pants. I am compelled to send them home, many of them at once, some to Harrisburg, some to Philadelphia, one to Indiana; and, if not otherwise directed by telegraph, I shall send to the place of muster, to which I request rolls may be sent, and Captain Hastings, Major Ruff, and Captain Wharton ordered to muster them out. They cannot march, and, unless a paymaster goes to them, they will be indecently clad, and have just cause of complaint.
>
> "R. PATTERSON,
> "Major-General, Commanding.
>
> "ADJUTANT-GENERAL U. S. ARMY,
> "Washington, D. C."

I succeeded then in detaining Johnston up to the afternoon of Thursday, the 18th, and no portion of his force arrived on the field of battle at Manassas until the afternoon of Sunday, the 21st, so that Johnston was kept from joining Beauregard not only on "Tuesday," or, "the early part of next week," but during the entire week. That the battle of Manassas was by that time fought and won by our troops I had no doubt. General Scott had telegraphed me on Wednesday, the 17th:

> "McDowell's first day's work has driven the enemy beyond Fairfax Court-house; the Junction will probably be carried to-morrow."

So that knowing Johnston to be still in my front, and that it would take him three days to reach Manassas, I felt confident that everything was progressing in accordance with the plans of the General-in-chief. Instead, however, of "the Junction being carried to-morrow" (Thursday), there was not even an attack made upon it until Sunday, the 21st, and then late in the day. Of all of which I was profoundly ignorant, never having received an intimation of it from any source whatever, so that I assumed, and had a right to assume, that if the General-in-chief told me he would fight on Tuesday, the 16th, and on the 17th had told me he had driven the enemy beyond a certain point, and would probably complete the operation on the next day, that it was his duty to inform me if he had not done it, otherwise, I must of course infer that he had done it. More especially, when it was in his power to have communicated with me by telegraph.

I informed the General-in-chief of Johnston's departure to join Beauregard in ample time to enable him to abstain from delivering battle, if he desired to do so.

I telegraphed as follows on the 20th of July:

"HEADQUARTERS DEPARTMENT OF PENNSYLVANIA,
CHARLESTOWN, VIRGINIA, July 20, 1861.

"With a portion of his force Johnston left Winchester, by the road to Millwood, on the afternoon of the 18th; his whole force 32,500.

"R. PATTERSON,
"Major-General, Commanding.
"COLONEL E. D. TOWNSEND,
"A. A. G. U. S. A., Washington, D. C."

In this connection, and to show the disposition of "the Committee on the Conduct of the War" towards myself, I will mention an incident which occurred in regard to this despatch in the House of Representatives. General Scott himself acknowledges the receipt of it in his commentary on my testimony. That I had filed this despatch with the Committee was well known by John Covode of Pennsylvania, and D. W. Gooch of Massachusetts, for both spoke of it when I handed it in, and Mr. Covode observed that he knew the fact, as he had heard it from several persons; and yet both afterwards denied the existence of it, as may be seen by reference to the Daily Globe of 15th February, 1862, during a debate in Congress, when Mr. Blair of Missouri was censuring the General-in-chief for forcing the Battle of Bull Run, without having my army to join General McDowell's after it was known that Johnston had come down. Mr. Blair said:

"I wish to state that it was well known to the General commanding the United States army, that General Johnston with his forces had eluded Patterson and was present at that fight at the beginning of it. I want to state that it was well known by despatches from General Patterson himself, and that when this information came here, the President of the United States went to General Scott and protested against the army proceeding against Bull Run and Manassas, but General Scott insisted upon its being done. And that whole defeat of the American army there occurred with the full knowledge of this fact upon the part of the General in command, and when they still insisted upon marching upon Manassas, they did it with the full knowledge that Beauregard had been reinforced by Johnston, and *against the protest of the President of the United States.* That, sir, is the fact in reference to this matter. It is a fact that I stated in the special session of Congress. It was not denied then, it cannot be denied now.

"Mr. Covode. Do I understand the gentleman to say that General Patterson had telegraphed General Scott that Johnston had eluded him?

"Mr. Blair of Missouri. Yes, sir, on Friday or Saturday preceding the Battle of Bull Run.

"Mr. Covode. Well, Mr. Speaker, I cannot explain the matter, but I simply say to the gentleman from Missouri, that he is mistaken.

"Mr. Blair of Missouri. And the gentleman from Missouri says he is not mistaken. He knows as much in reference to this matter as the gentleman upon the Committee on the Conduct of the War, and has as high authority for what he states as the gentleman from Pennsylvania.

"Mr. Covode. I say that General Patterson never telegraphed any such thing to General Scott. . . . .

"Mr. Gooch. Do I understand the gentleman from Missouri to say that General Scott had the information from General Patterson that General Johnston had eluded him?

"Mr. Blair. Yes, sir, General Patterson.

"Mr. Gooch. I think the gentleman from Missouri is mistaken, and I would like to know on what authority he makes the statement.

"Mr. Blair. I know the fact. I desire to be as particular as positive. I know that the President and General Scott were advised of the fact by General Patterson himself.

"Mr. Bingham. When?

"Mr. Blair. I have stated several times. It was on Friday or Saturday previous to the battle. The President went to General Scott. I do not know whether he protested or not, but he suggested the propriety of waiting until General Patterson could be here with his forces, inasmuch as Johnston had eluded him. General Scott disregarded the wish and advice of the President on the subject. The military commander at that time, sir, brought upon us the disaster which befell our arms at Bull Run.

"Mr. Gooch. I think it possible that the President of the United States might have been in possession of the information to which the gentleman from Missouri refers, but I think, I know that he did not receive the information from General Patterson in any way whatever. The fact may have been telegraphed to the papers in Philadelphia, and from there may have been telegraphed here, *but I do not think that General Patterson ever sent it to him or to anybody else in Washington.*

"Mr. Covode. . . . In regard to the telegraphic despatch from General Patterson. I have been astonished that the gentleman from Missouri has persisted so long in argument with gentlemen on this floor, who had their hands tied, and were not in a position to answer him, when it was boldly asserted by them that that despatch was never sent by General Patterson."

Here is a series of assertions and contradictions. Mr. Blair, an independent member, anxious to vindicate the truth of history, asserts facts to the best of his knowledge, and although not a member of the Committee, nor having seen the evidence or documents, yet, every word he utters is truth.

Messrs. Covode and Gooch, partisan members of the Committee, with all the evidence and documents in their possession, positively assert that which was entirely false, in their extreme anxiety to make me the scapegoat. I had informed the Committee on the Conduct of the War, Messrs. Covode and Gooch being members, and both present at the time (see *Report*, vol. ii, p. 97), that on the 20th July I telegraphed General Scott as follows:

"With a portion of his force Johnston left Winchester by the road to Millwood on the afternoon of the 18th."

It so chanced that one of my staff, Major Craig Biddle, was present in the House of Representatives at this debate. Major Biddle, knowing that I had so informed General Scott, and that the assertions of Covode and Gooch were untrue, telegraphed to me for a copy of my telegram to General Scott, which on receipt he placed in the hands of Mr. Blair, who again brought the subject before the House.

I quote from the Congressional Globe:

"Mr. Blair of Missouri. . . . In July last, or 1st of August, when I first spoke upon the subject in this House, for the purpose of putting that responsibility where it belonged, I stated what I knew to be a fact, and reiterated that fact on Friday last, that the General in command of the army knew that General Johnston had eluded General Patterson, and left Winchester to reinforce General Beauregard at Manassas. That is what I said, but it seemed that gentlemen upon the other side were so full of some secret they had got in committee, that they at once raised this side issue with me, as to whether General Patterson sent the despatch or not.

"Mr. Gooch. If the gentleman will permit me to interrupt him, I desire to say that, so far as I am concerned, I desire to raise no side issue with him, so far as the main question is concerned, as to this information being received by the authorities here. I did, however, desire to correct the gentleman in reference to his statement that General Patterson furnished this information."

(That is, Mr. Gooch was quite willing that Mr. Blair should say that the authorities were informed of the fact, but it would not answer their purpose to let it be known that General Patterson had given the information.)

"Mr. Blair said: I believed at the time that this information came direct from General Patterson to the General in command here; but that General Scott received the information there is no earthly doubt. Nor is there any doubt that the President suggested to General Scott the propriety of waiting for General Patterson's army, in order to support the column of General McDowell. I have no doubt of that fact, for I have knowledge of it. It is of no importance whether

General Patterson sent the information or not, but it appears from the letter which I hold in my hand that I am correct, and that General Patterson did send a despatch to General Scott on the subject. I received the letter from a gentleman with whom I am very well acquainted, and I will read it for the information of the House:

"WASHINGTON, February 16th, 1862.
"MY DEAR COLONEL:

"I inclose a copy of a despatch which has been forwarded to me by General Patterson. It, as well as my own recollection, fully confirms the statement made by you in the House, that General Patterson on the 20th of July communicated to the headquarters of the army at Washington the intelligence that Johnston had, with a portion of his force, left Winchester by the road to Millwood. This despatch was given in evidence before the Investigating Committee, as appears by its record. General Patterson's force at Martinsburg was eighteen thousand two hundred men.

"Very sincerely yours,
"CRAIG BIDDLE."

(*Despatch.*)

"HEADQUARTERS DEPARTMENT OF PENNSYLVANIA,
CHARLESTOWN, VIRGINIA, July 20, 1861.

"With a portion of his force, Johnston left Winchester by the road to Millwood on the afternoon of the 18th. His whole force thirty-five thousand two hundred.

"R. PATTERSON,
"Major-General, Commanding.
"COLONEL E. D. TOWNSEND,
"Assistant Adjutant-General U. S. Army,
"Washington, D. C."

This debate gives a fair sample of the "reliable information" which members of this Committee were enabled, by their position, to foist upon the public, and which not every one is so lucky as to be able to prove utterly mendacious by their own record, before the very body that appointed them.

No one acquainted with the country needs to be told that my movement from Martinsburg to Charlestown was in no respect a retreat or withdrawal from the enemy.

When I arrived at Charlestown, and was about to advance from that point, the difficulties which I anticipated from the expiration of the time of service of the regiments under my command culminated. I have shown that my requisition on the Governor of Pennsylvania for three years' troops in May had been countermanded. I, therefore, having none but three months' troops under my command, in my communications to the General-in-chief never failed to urge the danger of acting just as their terms of service were expiring. On the 20th of June I had used to General Scott (*Report on the Conduct of the War*, vol. ii, p. 126) the following emphatic, and, I may say, prophetic language:

"I beg to remind the General-in-chief that the period of service of nearly all the troops here will expire within a month, and that if we do not meet the enemy with them, we will be in no condition to do so for three months to come."

Yet, with this fact perfectly well known, the attack on Manassas was delayed until the 21st of July. On the 16th, I had said (p. 132):

"I have to report that the term of service of a very large portion of this force will expire in a few days. From an undercurrent expression of feeling, I am confident that many will be inclined to lay down their arms the day their time expires. With such a feeling existing, any active operations towards Winchester cannot be thought of, until they are replaced by three years' men."

And on the 17th, 18th, and 19th, the same thing (*Report*, p. 92).

What made the matter still worse, was an order, published at Washington, which had become known to the command, directing that all volunteers in service should be returned to their homes in time to be mustered out at the expiration of their term of service. This was in accordance with the law on the subject, but no reinforcements were sent me to replace the troops of which a literal compliance with this order would have entirely stripped me.

My time after this was employed in sending off the troops under my command, until, on the 25th of July, I was relieved by General Banks.

This is a plain unexaggerated statement of the whole of my operations.

· I think that I have shown :

" 1st. That I have always courted an investigation of any charge that could be made against me.

" 2d. That my whole course was entirely approved by the officers attached to my column, whom I was instructed to consult.

" 3d. That I complied with every order issued to me.

" 4th. That I kept Johnston from joining Beauregard, not only on the day I was directed to do so, but for five days afterwards.

" 5th. That I was never informed that the battle had not been fought at the time indicated, though within reach of a telegraph, but on the contrary, the only despatch received convinced me that the battle had been fought.

" 6th. That for the delay in fighting it I was in nowise responsible.

"7th. That the General-in-chief, when I told him I was not strong enough, in my opinion, to attack Johnston, could have ordered me to do so, if he differed from me, as I told him all the circumstances, and asked, 'Shall I attack?'

"8th. That I informed him that Johnston had gone to General Beauregard, and he himself, in his comments on my testimony (see page 241, vol. ii, *Conduct of the War*), admits that he knew it before delivering battle on the 21st of July."

Of the testimony taken before the Committee on the Conduct of the War, relative to the operations of my column, it is unnecessary for me to make a minute examination. The documentary evidence and the best informed witnesses sustain me in all that I have here presented. Some of the witnesses were honest, well-meaning gentlemen, but acquainted neither with my orders, my force, the amount of my transportation, nor anything which would enable them to form a fair judgment. Some were without any military knowledge or experience. To notice their strictures minutely would be tedious to the reader, and seems to be superfluous.

These reflections do not apply to the remarks of General Scott, which I desire to notice with all the consideration to which anything coming from him is entitled. His statement, sent to the Committee, is as follows:

"NEW YORK, March 31, 1862.

"On the statement of Major-General Patterson, submitted by him as evidence to the Honorable the Committee of the House of Representatives on the Conduct of the War, I beg leave to remark:

"1. That his statement, one hundred and forty-eight long pages, closely and indistinctly written, has been before me about forty-eight hours, including a Sunday when I was too much indisposed to work or to go to church; that I cannot write or read at night nor at any time, except by short efforts, and that I have been entirely without help.

" 2. That, consequently, I have read but little of the statement and voluminous documents appended, and have but about two hours left for comments on that little.

" 3. The documents (mainly correspondence between General Patterson and myself) are badly copied, being hardly intelligible in some places from the omission and change of words.

" 4. General Patterson was never ordered by me, as he seems to allege, to attack the enemy without a probability of success; but on several occasions he wrote as if he were assured of victory. For example: June 12th, he says he is 'resolved to conquer, and will risk nothing;' and July 4th, expecting supplies the next day, he adds, as soon as they 'arrive I shall advance to Winchester, to drive the enemy from that place.' Accordingly he issued orders for that movement on the 8th, next called a council of war, and stood fast at Martinsburg.

" 5. But although General Patterson was never specifically ordered to attack the enemy, he was certainly told, and expected, even if with inferior numbers, to hold the rebel army in his front on the alert, and to prevent it from reinforcing Manassas Junction, by means of threatening manœuvres and demonstrations, results often obtained in war with half numbers.

" 6. After a time, General Patterson moved upon Bunker Hill, and then fell off upon Charlestown, whence he seems to have made no other demonstration that did not look like a retreat out of Virginia. From that movement Johnston was at liberty to join Beauregard with any part of the army of Winchester.

" 7. General Patterson alludes, with feeling, to my recall from him, back to Washington, after the enemy had evacuated Harper's Ferry, of certain troops sent to enable him to take that place, but the recall was necessary to prevent the

Government and capital from falling into the enemy's hands. His inactivity, however, from that cause need not have been more than temporary, for he was soon reinforced up to, at least, the enemy's maximum number in the Winchester valley, without leading to a battle, or even a reconnoissance in force.

"8. He also often called for batteries and rifled cannon beyond our capacity to supply at the moment, and so in respect to regular troops, one or more regiments. He might as well have asked for a brigade of elephants. Till some time afterwards, we had for the defence of the Government and its capital but a few companies of regular foot and horse, and not half the number of troops, including all descriptions, if the enemy had chosen to attack us.

"9. As connected with this subject, I hope I may be permitted to notice the charge made against me on the floor of Congress, that I did not stop Brigadier-General McDowell's movement upon Manassas Junction, after I had been informed of the reinforcement sent thither from Winchester, though urged to do so by one or more members of the Cabinet.

"Now, it was, at the reception of that news, too late to call off the troops from the attack, and, besides, though opposed to the movement at first, we had all become animated and sanguine of success; and it is not true that I was urged by anybody in authority to stop the attack, which was commenced as early, I think, as the 18th of July.

"10. I have but time to say that, among the disadvantages under which I have been writing are these: I have not had within reach one of my own papers, and not an officer who was with me at the period in question.

"Respectfully submitted to the Committee.

"WINFIELD SCOTT.

"NEW YORK, March 31, 1862."

General Scott's infirmities, thus detailed by himself, entitle him to the most sincere sympathy. His admission that he has been able to read but little of the "documents (mainly correspondence between General Patterson and myself)," while it detracts very much from his comments upon them, is certainly creditable to his frankness. If too numerous to read, they must surely be too numerous to remember, especially by one who, at the time they were written or received, was occupied in the direction of other important military operations.

The General admits that I was "never ordered to attack without a probability of success."

In fact I was never *ordered to attack* at all, and as I did not see a probability of success, nor did any of the officers he had attached to my command and instructed me to consult, I claim that I was right not to attack the enemy's intrenched position at Winchester.

Every despatch I ever received impressed upon me, not the necessity of striking a blow, or making a bold dash upon the enemy, but the exercise of the greatest caution; to risk nothing, and never to give battle without a well-ascertained superiority. All felt that the first blow should be a decisive one, and that any success by the rebels would prove, as it did, an encouragement to years of resistance. After actually issuing the order for an attack on Winchester, I yielded reluctantly to the belief of my inability to do what I hoped, on the clearest evidence, and upon the judgment of those entitled to be consulted.

I did, with greatly inferior numbers, "hold the rebel army in my front on the alert," and I did prevent it from reinforcing Manassas Junction, by means of threatening manœuvres and demonstrations "as ordered by my military superior," not only on the day General Scott desired me to do so, but for five days afterwards. That no advantage was taken of this was not my fault. That the General-in-chief should cast any reflection upon the movement to Charlestown, is certainly singular, as he had himself ordered me to go there (*ante*, p. 68), and I had told him the precise day I was going and the route, *via* Bunker Hill, which I should take (*ante*, p. 70). After my arrival in Charlestown the expiration of the term of service of most of my troops prevented any further demonstration. The fact that they would not in any number remain beyond their term of service at my request, created remark at the time, but as every commander who has since tried the experiment, has met with similar experience, I do not deem it necessary to give any of the details of my efforts to detain them.

I regretted the recall of certain troops, just as I was partially across the Potomac, as it left me entirely without artillery. If it was necessary to paralyze my force to save Washington, I have no complaint to make. But after it was done, I do object to being blamed for the temporary delay occasioned by it.

I did subsequently move, two days after receiving a single battery of six guns, and crossed the Potomac with less than 11,000 men, in the face of a force proved by the official report of General Johnston to be greatly my superior, and having, according to my information, 24 pieces of artillery.

Whether batteries and cannon could or could not be supplied me, I shall not discuss. As my adversary had,

IN THE VALLEY OF THE SHENANDOAH. 91

as he admits, at least 16 pieces of field artillery, together with heavy siege guns, I think no one will blame me for my attempts, ineffectual though they were, to obtain some additions to my six. My siege train when near Winchester consisted of one 30-pounder, one 24-pounder, and an old eight-inch howitzer.

General Scott scorns to avail himself of the misstatements of the Committee, but frankly admits that he received the intelligence of Johnston's approach, but determined to fight the battle of Bull Run in spite of it. How absurd is it then to attribute the disaster of that day to the *unexpected* arrival of Johnston. It was known, but evidently deemed of small moment; so great was the confidence at Washington, that they would not wait until I could come up. They deemed, and public opinion supported them in it, that their force was perfectly irresistible against everything that the rebels could oppose to it. To use General Scott's own words:

"Though opposed to the movement at first, we had all become animated and sanguine of success."

I did not write to General Scott "as if assured of victory," though repeatedly declaring my readiness to assault Winchester if ordered by him to do so. I said nothing in my reports to foster the too sanguine expectation of success - which precipitated the attack of McDowell, while from my position it was impossible for me to co-operate with him. That my estimate of the difficulties of an advance in the Shenandoah Valley, with the three months' volunteers, was not exaggerated, sufficiently appears from the ill success that has since attended the movements, in that direction, of more experienced troops, successively commanded by Generals Stone, Frémont, Banks, Miles, Milroy, Sigel, Wallace, and Hunter. The first successful campaign there since I relinquished the command was made very recently, by General Sheridan, at the head of a veteran army, after first meeting serious reverses.

General Scott, in his recent Autobiography, has added nothing to his criticisms on this campaign, further than to say, in speaking of the attack on Vera Cruz:

" Several Generals and Colonels, among them Major-General Patterson, an excellent second in command, notwithstanding his failure as chief on the Shenandoah in 1861, solicited the privilege of leading storming parties."

While I am duly grateful for this compliment to my services in Mexico, I must protest against the assertion that I acted "as Chief on the Shenandoah in 1861." I was a subordinate, without knowing the plan of my principal. I was ordered to co-operate in a movement which was not—and I was not informed of its postponement—made at the time indicated. When I was in a condition to move into Virginia, and had actually crossed the Potomac, I was ordered back, and told " to keep within my limits, until I could satisfy the General-in-chief I ought to go beyond them." When I presented my plan to go to Leesburg, it was disapproved. When I asked for instructions, they were not given. My movements were regulated by telegraphic despatches, received from day to day and hour to hour, and I never was invested with the dignity of "Chief," until it became expedient to make me responsible for the failure of the campaign.

It will appear by an examination of the testimony before the Committee on the Conduct of the War, that the arrival of General Johnston at Manassas was one of the very least of the causes of General McDowell's defeat.

In answer to questions put by the Committee, the following evidence was given.

General J. B. Richardson:

"I moved back to see what had become of the New York 12th, on the left. It had probably taken as much as twenty minutes to go through with this formation. I found, on arriving at the left, parts of two companies of the New York 12th, about sixty men altogether, retreating outside of the woods, carrying along a few wounded. I asked what the matter was and where they were going. They said the regiment was all killed, and they were falling back; the regiment had fallen back, those that were not killed. Says I, 'What are you running for? there is no enemy here. I cannot see anybody at all. Where is your Colonel?' They knew nothing about it. The men knew nothing about any of their officers. I could not find any officers with the men at all, I believe.

"Question. Why was it concluded to fight that battle on Sunday, without any knowledge of where Patterson and his men were, and of the position of Johnston? Did you know at the time where they were? I will ask that first.

"Answer. Yes, sir. I knew General Johnston was on our right before we moved from there at all."

General Richardson further says that if he had captured certain batteries on Thursday night, which he could have done, there would have been no serious fight;

that reinforcements from Richmond under General Davis, and from Winchester under General Johnston, came during Friday and Saturday nights, and he gives very clear reasons for the defeat at Bull Run. He says:

"There is another thing I would like to say. From what we have learned since, the enemy handled every reserve they had, *whereas our reserves were not handled at all.* The three brigades of reserves, Blenker's, Davis's, and mine, that were on the field that day, and Runyon's reserve, which was at Fairfax Station, six miles off, I believe, and not handled at all, make 24,000 who were useless, *whereas the enemy handled all their reserves.* This is nothing new. I said the same that night."

General Richardson adds:

"We marched 50,000 men and 49 pieces of artillery, of which we saved 35 pieces."

Major-General Heintzelman attributes the loss of the battle to the delay in bringing it on, and to improper disposition of the troops. Tyler's division, having but the *shortest* distance to go, was ordered to move first. Hunter's, which had the *longest* distance to go, followed Tyler's; and Heintzelman says:

"I think if we had reversed it, let Hunter go first, then let me follow him, and then Tyler follow me, that delay at Centreville would not have occurred.

"Question to General Heintzelman. What in your opinion really led to the disaster of that day?

"Answer. It is hard to tell. There were a number of causes. In the first place, the delay of Friday and Saturday at Centreville was an efficient cause. Another cause was the three hours lost at Centreville on Sunday morning."

Major-General Franklin:

"Question by the Chairman. I have always wondered that the battle was fought then, when it was, after it was understood in the army that Johnston had come down, contrary to the expectation which was entertained, that Patterson would hold him in check.

"Answer. I will tell you what suggested itself to me, when I got to Bull Run, and that is: we ought to have encamped at the fine hills there, and waited there overnight, and got up early in the morning, when we could have whipped them.

"Question by the Chairman. It has always seemed to me that, when you knew that Johnston had come down, you should have got twenty-five thousand men from here, and as many more, perhaps, from Fortress Monroe, and then you would have had the thing sure. I always wondered why that was not done when Patterson had not held Johnston in check, as it was understood he would do.

"The witness. Patterson's officers give a very good account of him. He knew nothing about what the army was to do. He supposed the battle had come off on Tuesday, and knew nothing about what was really doing.

"The Chairman. It strikes me that it was a great fault that so important a circumstance was not understood before the battle was begun.

"The witness. I think that if we had stopped at Sudley's stream they would have fought us in the morning, but we would have fought them on our own ground, and would have whipped them.

"The Chairman. They would then have lost the benefit of all their batteries. I have always wondered at you going into that fight there, when you should really have got reinforcements of twenty to thirty thousand more men.

"The witness. I think it would have been an advisable

plan to have stopped there at Bull Run. We would probably have had to fight about the same time, but then we should have fought on our own ground, and should have had a better position than they could have got. We could have got a beautiful position."

From the testimony of General Wadsworth:

"Question. What is your opinion as to the result of that battle, had the provisions and transportation been brought up on Thursday, and the battle fought on Friday morning, instead of Sunday?

"Answer. We would have walked over the field. Johnston is regarded by our officers as much superior to Beauregard; as much the ablest officer in this army. All the reports show that he had a great deal to do with the disposition of the enemy on that day."

General Henry W. Slocum:

"Question by Mr. Odell. You were in Hunter's division and rested at Centreville, did you not?

"Answer. Yes, sir.

"Question. Do you remember why it was you rested there an hour or an hour and a half on Sunday morning?

"Answer. I never understood that. I understood that there was some confusion among the troops ahead of us; somebody in the way, I understood. It was a very unfortunate resting spell.

"Question by Mr. Chandler. But for that you would have won the day?

"Answer. Yes, sir, I think so."

General William F. Barry:

"Question. Can you state to us what led to the rout of our army on the field that day?

"Answer. I think the principal cause was the uninstructed state of our troops. The troops were raw, many of the officers were indolent, and they did not behave themselves as they should have done on that day."

Further on, General Barry says:

"It was impossible to rally the Eleventh regiment, the Fire Zouaves. I rode in among them, and implored them to stand. I told them the guns would never be captured if they would only stand, but they seemed paralyzed; standing with their eyes and mouths wide open, and did not seem to hear me. I then reminded them of all the oaths they had sworn at Alexandria, after the death of Ellsworth, and that that was the best chance they would ever have for vengeance, but they paid no attention to what I said at all.

"Question. So far as the whole fight was concerned, the enemy had infinitely the advantage of our troops in position?

"Answer. Yes, sir, the ground was of their own selecting. I think if the battle had been fought at the hour it was expected to be fought, at $8\frac{1}{4}$ or $8\frac{1}{2}$ o'clock in the morning, we would have won it. There was a loss of three hours then, which I think had a very important effect on the success of the day. It enabled their fresh troops to get up; it prevented our turning their flank so completely as we would have done by surprise, for when our column halted the enemy discovered the direction we were going to take, and prepared for it; and, worse than that, the halting, the standing still, fatigued the men as much, if not more, than by marching that time.

"Question. So that our men were really very much exhausted when they went into the field?

"Answer. Yes, sir.

"Question. But if the battle had been fought three or four hours earlier, then Johnston's reserves would not have been up in time?

"Answer. I think the fate of that day would have been decided before they got upon the ground. I look upon that delay as the most unfortunate thing that happened. The troops that ought to have been out of the way were in the way before we could get to the turning-off point of the road."

General E. D. Keyes :

"Question by the Chairman. To what do you attribute the disaster of the day?

"Answer. To the want of ten thousand more troops. That is, I think if we had ten thousand more troops than we had to go into action, say at eleven o'clock in the morning, we should certainly have beaten them. I followed along down the stream, and Sherman's battery diverged from me, so that it left a wide gap between us, and ten thousand men could have come in between me and Sherman, which was the weak point in our line, &c.

"Question by the Chairman. Had it been known that Patterson had not detained Johnston, would it not have been imprudent to hazard a battle then anyhow?

"Answer. If it had been known that the thirty to forty thousand men that Johnston was said to have had, would have been upon us, it would have been impolitic to have made the attack on Sunday.

"Question by the Chairman. Even after the disaster, what prevented your making a stand at Centreville, and sending for reinforcements and renewing the fight there?

"Answer. I was not the Commander-in-chief.

"Question by the Chairman. Was there not a strong brigade on Centreville Heights that had not been in the engagement at all that day?

"Answer. There was a division there,—three brigades."

General John G. Barnard, chief engineer to General McDowell:

"Question by Chairman. Without going minutely into the matter, will you state concisely to what you attribute the disaster to our army in that battle?

"Answer. One of the influential causes was, I think, the

loss of time in getting underway the morning of the fight. The fact the repulse turned into a disastrous defeat, I attribute to the fact that our troops were all raw. General McDowell had not even time to see all his troops. They were brigaded only for the march, and put under officers whom the troops had not time to know, and who had no time to know the troops, &c.

"Question by the Chairman. You attribute the first bad phase of that battle to the fact that our troops did not get on the ground in time?

"Answer. Yes, sir. I think one hour's difference would have gained the battle. We had almost gained it as it was.

"Question. What caused that delay?

"Answer. There were two causes, distinct from each other. One was, that in the plan of the attack, General Tyler's division was to move first, &c. The second was, the much longer time it took for the column of Hunter to get around Sudley's Ford than we calculated for," &c.

Captain (now General) Charles Griffin:

In answer to the question of the Chairman, "Will you please inform us what, according to your best judgment, led to the disaster of that day?" replies at length, and gives as reason, that his battery, also the battery of Captain Ricketts, were put entirely too far in advance, in a wrong position and without an adequate support, with only the New York Fire Zouaves; that he took the position he was ordered to, against his judgment, saying, the Zouaves would not support him; saying, "I will go, but mark my words, they will not support us," and that when the firing began, the supports "broke and run," and the batteries were lost.

"Question by the Chairman. You say if your battery and

Ricketts' had been properly supported, it could not have been taken?

"Answer. If those eleven guns had been properly supported, I think the day would have been different, and I think that if we had not been moved on that point, and the Captains of the batteries had been allowed to exercise their own judgment, the day would have resulted differently.

"Question. Was it not necessary, in your advanced position, that you should have had the largest requisite number to support you?

"Answer. Yes, sir. In the first place, a battery should never have been sent forward to reconnoitre. That is a military mistake; of course I am only a Captain, and a great many would censure me for saying this, but it is so. It was the duty of the infantry to have gone forward and found out what the enemy were doing, and not to have sent the battery forward to find that out."

Further on he says (p. 174):

"My last words were, 'These Fire Zouaves will never support me.'

"Question. Why did you think that?

"Answer. I had seen them on the field in a state of disorganization, and I did not think they had the moral courage to fight. I do not think that any troops that will go through the country in a disorganized state, thieving and robbing, are brave men. I had no support all day long, with the exception that the New York 14th came to me when I was in my second or third position. An officer said, 'I have been ordered here to support you; where shall I go?' He went to a fence in rear of the batteries. I said, 'Don't go in rear of us, for you will stand a chance of being hit. If their batteries fire at me and don't hit me, it will pass over me and hit you.' They then went to one side, and when I saw them again they were falling back, every man for himself, about five hundred yards from me. That was the last I saw of that regiment that day.

"Question. You consider one of the errors, the serious error of the day, was the fact that the artillery was not properly supported by the infantry?

"Answer. Undoubtedly. I consider that the first great error that was committed that day was the sending these batteries forward without support.

"Question. These two errors you think led to the first and most important repulse of the day?

"Answer. I think these two errors led to the first and *the* repulse of the day."

Colonel Thomas A. Davies:

"Question. What led to the final defeat, as near as you could ascertain on the ground?

"Answer. I can tell you what I think is the cause of the whole defeat of that day. The troops were raw; the men had been accustomed to look to their Colonels as the only men to give them commands. They had never been taught the succession of officers, &c., &c. The officers did not themselves know what to do. They were themselves raw and green, &c., &c. That I think was the cause of many of the regiments returning from the field, not from any cowardice or fear of fighting, but because, having lost their Colonels, they supposed they were out of the battle. I consider that the great cause of our army being put in rout on the right wing.

"Question. What would have been the effect had you waited there at Centreville Heights, and rested your men a day or two, seeing that Johnston was down there, until Patterson's army had followed him there, and been ordered to turn their left?

"Answer. We should, undoubtedly, have won the battle.

"Question. Would you have had any difficulty in rallying your whole forces and holding your position on Centreville Heights, while you sent for Patterson, or for reinforcements from here and Fortress Monroe? Would you not have worsted the enemy in that way?

"Answer. We never should have been compelled to leave the place, with what troops I had under my command. I could have held my position there with the troops I had, which were, my brigade, Richardson's brigade, Blenker's brigade, and some batteries.

"Question. Was it not a terrible military blunder to come back to Washington in disorder?

"Answer. That is putting it rather strong. I should not like to say it was a military blunder.

"Question. Well, it was a mistake then?

"Answer. I think this: that we could have held our position there. There is no doubt about that.

"Question. Then you ought to have held it, ought you not?

"Answer. That is a matter I am not responsible for, &c.

"Question. Would it not have been easier to have defended Washington on Centreville Heights than to have come pellmell here to do it?

"Answer. I can answer that very readily. I think it would. There is no doubt about that."

General Daniel Tyler:

"Question by Chairman. Please give a brief and concise statement of what you saw there, and how the battle was conducted, &c., &c. Do this without questioning at first. I want to get particularly what, in your judgment, caused the disaster on that day.

"Answer. The first great trouble was the want of discipline and instruction in the troops. The troops needed that regimental and brigade instruction which would have enabled them to act together in masses to advantage.

"Question. Were there any more proximate causes than that?

"Answer. There was a great want of instruction and professional knowledge among the officers,—the company and regimental officers.

"Question. Why did you move first, as you were to move the shortest distance on the road?

"Answer. That was the order of march by General McDowell."

General Andrew Porter was asked the following leading question:

"Had Patterson detained Johnston in the valley of Winchester, so that no reinforcements would have been brought down by Johnston to Beauregard, what, in your opinion, would have been the result of that battle?

"Answer. Well, it might have ended one way or the other. Our troops could not stand the attacking of the enemy; they were played out quite early. The men were exhausted; somehow or other, they seemed to have no heart in the matter. The officers were more to blame than the men," &c., &c.

General William W. Averill:

"Question. What, in your judgment, caused the disaster of that day?

"Answer. They commenced, I presume, almost from the time we started from Arlington, from the other side of the river. There were a great many causes that combined to lose the day to us. The most apparent cause, however, at the time we first felt we were beaten, that we had to retire, and that we had felt for some time beforehand, was the want of concentration of the troops; the feeling that we ought to have had more men in action at one time.

"Question. The want of concentration in the field?

"Answer. Yes, sir. We crossed the Run with eighteen thousand men. I do not believe there were over six or eight thousand actually engaged at any one time.

"Question. Was not the nature of the battle-field such, that it was exceedingly difficult to bring a large body of men into action at any one time?

"Answer. I think it was about as fine a battle-field as

you could find between here and Richmond. I have no idea there was any better.

"Question. Was the field favorable for the movements and manœuvring of large bodies of men?

"Answer. One or two divisions of the size we had there could have manœuvred very well."

Further on, General Averill says (p. 214):

"There was the want of a headquarters somewhere on the field. All the staff officers who knew anything about the position of the enemy, had to act without orders."

General Ricketts:

"Question. Was it good generalship to order you to advance with your battery without more support than you had?

"Answer. Do you mean the one regiment?

"Question. Yes, sir, the Fire Zouaves you speak of.

"Answer. No, sir, I do not think it was, &c., &c.

"Question. Suppose that battle could have been fought two weeks before it was fought, what would have been the result?

"Answer. I believe if we had fought it even two days before, we would have walked over the field.

"Question. As a military man, to what circumstances do you attribute our disaster on that day?

"Answer. I impute it to the want of proper officers among the volunteers.

"Question. Do you mean the Colonels and Generals?

"Answer. I mean throughout. I cannot say particular Colonels and particular Captains, because many of them were excellent. But, as a general rule, many of the officers were inferior to the men themselves," &c.

These extracts from the testimony of fourteen general officers, out of eighteen examined, nearly all of them experienced and distinguished in the service, show that there was no difficulty whatever in ascertaining the true cause of defeat at Bull Run. Each gave his opinion as to what caused the defeat on that day, all going to show conclusively that the defeat was attributable to the following causes:

1st. The failure of General McDowell to attack Manassas, as he could have done, before the 21st of July, prior to the arrival of the enemy's reinforcements, instead of on that day, after they had arrived.

2d. The delay of the whole army for several hours on the 21st of July.

3d. The throwing of two of our batteries to the front, beyond support, thus causing their capture.

4th. The failure to have within supporting distance, and to bring into action at the critical moment, the ample reserves of that army, which were more than double the number of my entire command.

5th. The want of discipline in the troops.

In the face of this testimony, the Committee assert in their report:

"That the principal cause of the defeat on that day was, the failure of General Patterson to hold the forces of Johnston in the Valley of the Shenandoah."

Had the arrival of Johnston, five days after the time I was directed to hold him, had the effect attributed to it, common fairness should have induced the Committee to say, not that it was my failure to hold Johnston, but that it was the delay in fighting the battle of Bull Run that was the principal cause of the defeat of General McDowell.

I have thus thrown together, as concisely as I could, the facts bearing on my case. It has been necessary to refer to many documents and papers, the perusal of which will be tedious, and even when read, not so satisfactory to the unmilitary reader as the opinion upon them by competent and intelligent officers. The present Major-General George H. Thomas, whose reputation as a soldier and a man is second to none, and who served under me during my whole campaign, in a letter received a few months ago, after an experience of three years of most arduous service, thus writes:

"HEADQUARTERS DEPARTMENT OF THE CUMBERLAND,
BEFORE ATLANTA, GA., Aug. 8th, 1864.

"MY DEAR GENERAL:

"Your favor of the 16th July, was only received a few days since, owing doubtless to the irregularities of the mails to the front. In the council of war at Martinsburg, I in substance advised an advance towards Winchester, at least as far as Bunker Hill, and if your information, after the army reached Bunker Hill, led you to believe that Johnston still occupied Winchester in force, then to shift our troops over to Charlestown, as that move would place our communications with our depot of supplies in safety, and still threaten and hold Johnston at Winchester, which I understand was all that you were expected or required to do. I should have advised a direct advance on Winchester, but for the character of the troops composing your army. They were all, with the exception of a couple of squadrons of the Second U. S. Cavalry and two batteries of regular artillery, three months' men, and their term of service would expire in a few days. Judging of them as of other volunteer troops, had I been their commander, I should not have been willing to risk them in a heavy battle, coming off within a few days of the expiration of their service.

"I have always believed, and have frequently so expressed myself, that your management of the three months' campaign was able and judicious, and was to the best interests of the service, considering the means at your disposal, and the nature of the troops under your command.

"With much respect and esteem, I remain, General,
"Very sincerely and truly yours,
"GEORGE H. THOMAS,
"Major-General U. S. V.
"MAJOR-GENERAL ROBERT PATTERSON,
"Philadelphia, Pa."

I also take great pride in presenting other testimonials, from officers who were familiar with the events as they occurred:

Letter from Major-General W. H. Keim:

"SURVEYOR-GENERAL'S OFFICE, STATE OF PENNSYLVANIA,
HARRISBURG, PA., Nov. 22d, 1861.

"MY DEAR GENERAL:

"I read your vindication of the campaign in Virginia, delivered at the First Troop festival, and believe it places your action in the proper light, and enlightens the public upon a subject which is little known to the people. I know that you had the advice and support of the regular army officers, as well as those of the volunteer service. The difficulties under which we labored, of men called out for three months, a serious evil; the short supplies of transportation, and the difficulty to keep up the subsistence, are not known to the army at this matured state of affairs, and can hardly be fully appreciated by any persons not connected with military movements on a large scale. I had the pleasure of an interview with the President a few weeks since, when, in speaking of my connection with your column, I took occasion to speak freely of the injustice done to you and your command, enumerated the trials and obstacles thrown in our way, and the folly of attacking an intrenched force with equal or inferior forces. I have no doubt time will vindicate and do justice to all.

"Yours, very truly,
" W. H. KEIM.

" MAJOR-GENERAL PATTERSON."

Letter from Colonel Richard A. Oakford:

"SCRANTON, December 4th, 1861.

" MAJOR-GENERAL R. PATTERSON.

" DEAR SIR : By reason of a lame hand, I have been unable for some time past to use my pen ; with the returning use of my hand, I cannot resist the desire to express my gratification that you have (at the supper of the First City Troop), seen a suitable time to defend yourself in part, against the false and unjust charges made against your strategy in Virginia.

" Living as I do in a part of Pennsylvania which is from circumstances closely connected with New York, and drawing most of its newspaper opinions from that city, I have found it difficult to disabuse the minds of my neighbors, of the false opinions they had received through the New York press.

" Your speech has had a good effect. I hope you will, when a fitting time arrives, publish all the orders, &c., connected with the movements of your *corps d'armée*, feeling well assured that when the public are aware of all the facts, that you will not only be exculpated from all censure, but that all your moves will be not only approved, but applauded.

" With best wishes, yours truly,
" RICHARD A. OAKFORD,
" Late Colonel, Commanding 15th Reg't P. V."

From Major-General James S. Negley.

"HEADQUARTERS NEGLEY'S BRIGADE,
CAMP NEVIN, November 24th, 1861.
"MAJOR-GENERAL ROBERT PATTERSON,
"Philadelphia.

"DEAR GENERAL: I read your speech at the Continental with much pleasure. While I deeply regretted the necessity of an old officer and well-tried friend of the Union having to vindicate his honor and patriotism at a festive board, I hope your words have reached the ears of an impartial public, who will now be willing to do you justice. I think there is no longer a necessity to blame the weak to shelter the strong.

"My staff join me in offering you their congratulations, and sincere wishes for your good health and continued prosperity, and assure you that you still have our friendship as warmly as when on the banks of the Potomac, and only regret that you are not with us.

"I have the honor to remain yours, very truly,
"JAMES S. NEGLEY."

Also a letter from Colonel (now General) George H. Gordon, formerly of the Regular army:

"HEADQUARTERS SECOND MASSACHUSETTS REGIMENT,
FREDERICK, MD., December 22d, 1861.
"GENERAL ROBERT PATTERSON,
"Philadelphia.

"MY DEAR SIR: Your letter of the 20th inst. reached me yesterday. It is with pleasure I reply. You are aware there are many facts known to me only as common rumor, in relation to your movement from Martinsburg to Bunker Hill, thence to Harper's Ferry, Virginia, such as the actual information you received as to when General McDowell was to give battle, and from whom you received it, also as to the number of the rebels at Winchester, their armament, defensive works, &c. Of these subjects, so vital in forming an exact conclusion, I have, as said before, no information but general rumor. I believe the rebels have never given us either their number at Winchester, the number or calibre of their artillery, or the nature and extent of their fortifications; if they have, I think you can accept their statements as conclusive. If it agrees with or is larger than your estimate at Bunker Hill, to have attacked Winchester with the force and armament you had would, in my judgment, have been bad generalship, would have been followed by certain defeat, with terrible loss of life. I again have to regret that the few days intervening between my arrival at Martinsburg, Virginia, where I joined your column, and the day you marched towards Winchester, did not give me an opportunity of better informing myself of the number and nature of the troops under your command. I joined you on Thursday, the 11th day of July, 1861, and marched as one regiment of your column on the Monday following, the 15th. From my own observation, and from what was told me by officers generally, I believed your force to consist almost entirely of those whose time, in a large majority of the regiments, was about expiring. I also believed, from what I heard, that my own was the only three years' regiment under your command. Much of your force, indeed I can except few regiments, I found more in rags than uniforms, and quite indifferent to discipline; some regiments appeared more like mobs than soldiers. As to the numbers of your column, I had been led to believe that it varied from thirty to forty thousand, but was astonished to learn from your Adjutant-General, now General Porter, commanding a division in the Army of the Potomac, that you had less than twenty thousand men under your command. When we left Martinsburg *en route* to Winchester, it was the prevailing opinion among all officers of rank that you had been informed McDowell would engage the rebels near Manassas on the 15th or 16th of July at farthest. For one, I placed implicit confidence in the report.

" On Monday night your whole column reached Bunker Hill, my regiment encamping on ground vacated that afternoon by the rebels, their fires still smoking, and evidences of their hasty retreat apparent. We were but a few miles from Winchester; the road thence was obstructed by logs; rebel pickets thrown out almost within sight and sound of our own. Here we remained until Wednesday morning, the 17th of July.

"At this time, from general rumor and from information received, I had no doubt of three facts: first, that a battle near Manassas had been fought by McDowell; second, that we had held the rebel leader at Winchester, Jo. Johnston, in check, and thus prevented his uniting his forces to those under the rebel Beauregard; third, that the rebels at Winchester numbered between thirty and forty thousand, supported by thirty or forty pieces of heavy siege artillery, and well posted behind strong fortifications. Then there seemed nothing more for your column to do but to establish itself on a different base-line than that from Williamsport to Martinsburg. A road over which supplies must be hauled by wagons from Hagerstown, Maryland, to Martinsburg, Virginia, thence by some mode of conveyance to any other portion of Virginia southward, is certainly not preferable to one which conveys all the way by rail, both in the loyal and rebel portion of the country. If we could establish ourselves at Harper's Ferry, to operate in the Shenandoah Valley and southward, between the Blue Ridge and the Potomac, there can be but one opinion of its military propriety, when it is known that the rebels had evacuated all the region north of Winchester, and that opinion must be favorable to you.

"You thus, on Wednesday, the 18th of July, moved your column, of less than twenty thousand, with all its encumbering wagon train, by flank, around Winchester, reaching Charlestown, Virginia, on the line of rail from Harper's Ferry to Winchester, Virginia, late in the afternoon of the same day. None doubted that we were risking much in making the detour.

"An exasperated force of rebels, largely outnumbering our own, with metal heavier and more numerous, would not, we supposed, permit us to get between them and the sources of our supplies, would not permit us to hold the key to the

Shenandoah Valley and the Valley of the Potomac, without at least fighting a severe battle, and seeking compensation for the loss, which we supposed we had occasioned them by preventing a junction with the rebels opposite Washington. But the movement was made, and made with signal ability, each brigade ready at a moment's notice to throw itself into line of battle, to protect its train, and to manœuvre, as occasion might require. I felt, sir, on Wednesday night, that you had outwitted the rebel Johnston. On Thursday morning, the 18th of July, you discovered the expected battle opposite Washington had not been fought. We were now at Charlestown, Virginia, but about ten miles from Winchester, rebels and patriots occupying about the same relative position as at Bunker Hill, although we had greatly the advantage. If the rebel Jo. Johnston expected an attack from Bunker Hill side, and had fortified accordingly, we had obviously gained much by appearing on the opposite side of Winchester, with a paved road and a railroad from Charlestown to that place. He could, in my judgment, be as well checked by your column at Charlestown as at Bunker Hill, and unless he had been attacked from the latter place immediately after our arrival, and defeated or severely cut up, we gained much by going to Charlestown in opening a way for future subsistence and receiving, if needed, by rail, other forces. If you could not defeat or cut up the rebel Johnston, it was wise to place yourself in better communication with your rear. In this you were governed, as I have said, by your reconnoissance. On Thursday, the 18th of July, the day after your arrival at Charlestown, I knew of your intention (having learned that McDowell had not engaged the rebels up to that time) to advance on Winchester, the rebel Jo. Johnston then being there with his forces. On the morning of that day I had been ordered to issue three days' rations to my command for this movement, but during the afternoon I received orders to move with my regiment to Harper's Ferry, to hold that place. I knew, by common report, that, in furtherance of your plan to attack the rebel Johnston, you on Thursday and Friday, the 18th and 19th of July, made repeated efforts to induce your command (many regiments of which were then out of service) to remain with you for only a few days, while you advanced and held the rebels in Winchester, or give them battle if they had met you. I heard that you plead, entreated, and expostulated with regiments whose term of service had expired, but with few exceptions it availed nothing. I was informed that the number of your force with which you could, under these circumstances, have attacked the rebels, did not exceed seven or eight thousand men; with these, in my judgment, to have moved elsewhere than Harper's Ferry would have been folly.

"To sum it all up, it appears to me, writing from memory, after some six months have intervened, that if you had known that McDowell had not attacked the rebels, while you were at Bunker Hill, the question of whether you should have attacked Johnston depended upon your reconnoissance and means of information of his strength. The force of your reasoning, that you ought not to attack, is much more cogent, if your information was positive that McDowell would attack on Monday or Tuesday, the 15th or 16th of July, or if you were only ordered to hold Johnston in check during those days, for then you were holding him in check. Your movement to Charlestown, whether McDowell had attacked or not, was wise for reasons, *and also, that you were in better position to make the attack.* *You certainly lost nothing, as the rebel Johnston did not leave Winchester during your flank movement.* Your attempt to hold Johnston, when you learned at Charlestown, McDowell had not engaged the rebels, failed from causes not within your control. Men whose term of service had expired, would have fought no better at Bunker Hill than at Charlestown or Bull Run. I am very sure, attacks upon you would never have been made, for the course you pursued, had McDowell fought the battle of Manassas when you were informed and had the best of reasons for believing he was going to.

"If these statements, hurriedly thrown together, meet your conviction as arguments, I am happy to be able to furnish them. At the time, I heard none condemn you, but, my dear sir, when will man cease to be reviled by the ignorant and malicious?

"I am, very truly,
"Your obedient servant,
"GEORGE H. GORDON,
"Colonel Second Massachusetts Reg't."

From the gallant General Shields:

"WASHINGTON, D. C., Feb. 20, 1862.
"MY DEAR GENERAL:

"I long wished to write you, and write you as an old and true friend, who feels the full force of the injustice that has been attempted towards you, but I determined to wait until I could see what the Senate was disposed to do in my own case. Yesterday I was confirmed, after holding up my nomination for weeks. . . . .

"But your case was one of crying injustice. It was for the attacking army to wait until you could co-operate with them. They had the power to time their attack to your movements, but you had not the power to accommodate your movements to the attack. But, General, military men do you justice, and the country is beginning to do it; and for one I have never failed everywhere to cry shame upon the base treatment you have received, and now I don't hear a man, who has a particle of sense, who does not do the same. . . . . .

"Your sincere friend,
"JAMES SHIELDS.
"GENERAL ROBERT PATTERSON,
"Philadelphia."

From Colonel Gibson, a Regular officer of great distinction:

"HEADQUARTERS FORT DELAWARE, DEL.,
July 25, 1861.
"GENERAL:

"I am, my dear sir, acquainted with the nature of your service, and the difficulties opposed to you, in your recent campaign. It is impossible for an officer of ordinary intelligence, to refer to the disasters of this week, without reflecting upon the untimely and crude plans of offensive operations in which no commander could take part but as a victim. I make allusion to these matters only to assure you of my respect, and that I shall consider it fortunate to be under your command, with the able staff that served you, should you be called upon to take the field again.

"A. A. GIBSON,
"Captain Second Artillery, Commanding.
"MAJOR-GENERAL ROBERT PATTERSON,
"Philadelphia."

The following resolutions of two regiments, the Twenty-fourth and Fifteenth Pennsylvania, who served under me, and were ready to remain if required, it gives me great pleasure also to refer to.

"*Proceedings of a Meeting of the Field, Staff and Company Officers of the Twenty-fourth Regiment, Pennsylvania Volunteers, commanded by Colonel Joshua T. Owen, held at the Encampment near Charlestown, Virginia, on the 18th July, 1861.*

"*Whereas*, We, the officers of the Twenty-fourth Regiment Pennsylvania Volunteers, believing that in the contest in which we are now engaged is involved the maintenance of constitutional freedom, and being devotedly attached to the Government of the United States, because of the great blessings it confers alike upon rich and poor, native and foreign born citizens, and

"*Whereas*, A sense of duty as citizens induced us to take the field in defence of the Government, and

"*Whereas*, Major-General Robert Patterson has this day appealed to us as patriots, to prolong the period of our service, in order that he may maintain his present strategical position, without detriment to the cause. Therefore,

"*Resolved*, That having entire confidence in the capacity of our Commanding General as a soldier, and his integrity as a patriot, and admiring the skill with which he has advanced his column thus far without loss, or unnecessary delay, we will stand by him until our places are supplied by other troops."

Second, those of the Fifteenth Regiment, whose gallant Colonel, Richard A. Oakford, was killed on the battlefield of Antietam:

"HEADQUARTERS FIFTEENTH REGIMENT P. V.,
HARPER'S FERRY, July 24, 1861.

"At a meeting of the officers and men of the Fifteenth Regiment, held this evening, they expressed unanimously their approval of General Patterson's official administration, at the same time deeply regretting that his military judgment should be questioned, knowing as they do the superior force of the enemy in position, and the unavoidable circumstances which controlled the movements of this column. It is also painful to their feelings to find the many important but bloodless victories achieved by his command overlooked in the hasty opinion of the public.
"RICHARD A. OAKFORD,
"Colonel Commanding."

In the debate in Congress to which I have referred (*ante*, p. 79), the representative of the District where I live, the Hon: Charles J. Biddle, distinguished in the war with Mexico, and commanding at the beginning of this war, a body of State troops, addressed the House as follows:

"MR. BIDDLE. I ask the gentleman from Massachusetts to yield to me.
"MR. LOVEJOY. I object.
"MR. BIDDLE. I ask the gentleman from Illinois to with-

draw his objection. It can do him no harm to hear a few words from me on this subject.

"Mr. LOVEJOY. I withdraw my objection.

"Mr. GOOCH. I yield to the gentleman from Pennsylvania, but I take it for granted that if my time expires, that I shall be allowed two minutes after he has concluded.

"Mr. BIDDLE. I thank the gentleman.

"Mr. Speaker, General Patterson is my townsman and constituent, and I may assume to know as much of him as the gentleman from Tennessee. I have no personal knowledge of the movements of the column which he commanded in July last. I was at that time in the military service, but in another part of Virginia, within the limits of General McClellan's command. But I have personal knowledge of the character of General Patterson. In his command were many of my constituents, connections, and friends, and I never heard one of them mention him in other terms than those of respect and confidence. He had upon his staff some of the most distinguished officers of the Regular Army, now deservedly filling positions of great trust; he had on his staff men of high character from civil life. They were fully cognizant of General Patterson's conduct and motives; their characters are additional guarantees for his.

"I believe that no man, really cognizant of the facts, has ever brought any charge against him, and that the vague, baseless rumors that have been circulated to his disadvantage are but hearsay upon hearsay, like the statement of the gentleman from Tennessee. Upon the occasion before Martinsburg, a brilliant affair at that time, when our greater and more glorious victories had not eclipsed it, General Patterson's conduct was distinguished alike by military skill and personal intrepidity. All the contemporary accounts, verbal and published in the newspapers, from all sources, agreed in that.

"With respect to his character at an earlier period, in the war with Mexico, I would not offer my humble testimony; but I sent to the adjoining library and have had brought here the volume of reports, from which I can cite, under the clear and venerable name of Winfield Scott, the high testimony that was then borne to General Patterson's character as a soldier. At the siege of Vera Cruz, General Scott says that 'he can only enumerate the few who are isolated by rank or position, as well as by noble services.' He then mentions 'Major-General Patterson, second in command.' At Cerro Gordo, General Scott says:

"'Major-General Patterson left a sick-bed to share in the dangers and fatigues of the day, and after the surrender went forward to command the advanced forces towards Xalapa.'

"He also served during the war of 1812, as lieutenant and captain, in the Regular Army. Of course I had no contemporary knowledge of his services there; but I know that by those who had, he was esteemed as a soldier, even at that early period of his life.

"This statement I have felt bound to make in behalf of a man who is my constituent, and who, I believe, has been unjustly aspersed by vague rumors and suspicions, only too common, and gaining too easy credence with us. Let me add, however, that in so doing I take no part in the criticisms upon General Scott, for whom no man living entertains higher respect than I do." (*Congressional Globe*, Feb. 17, 1862.)

The numberless private communications, both verbal and written, which I have received, approving my course, I shall refer to no further than to say, that they will ever merit, as they have always received, my warmest gratitude.

INDEX.

INDEX.

	PAGE
Abercrombie, General, Brigade of, at Falling Waters,	47
at Council of War at Martinsburg,	52–55
opinion of Johnston's retreat,	57
report from Winchester, 1862,	62, 63
Annapolis, route through, established by Patterson,	27
Army, Patterson's, strength of, June 25th–29th,	43–47
" " July,	63
Johnston's " June,	43, 44
" " July,	57–62
Artillery, Patterson's amount of field, June 29th,	47
Johnston's " "	61
Patterson's " siege,	91
Johnston's " left at Winchester,	62
Averill, W. W. General, opinion of causes of defeat at Bull Run,	103, 104
Babcock, Lieutenant, U. S. A., at affair at Falling Waters,	49
repairs canal at Sandy Hook,	76
Baltimore, passage forced through,	27
Banks, N. P. General, relieves General Patterson July 25th,	85
Barnard, J. G. General, opinion of causes of defeat at Bull Run,	98, 99
Barry, W. F. " " " " " "	96, 97
Beckwith, Captain, U. S. A., at council at Martinsburg,	52–55
opinion of Johnston's retreat,	57
Berkley County, citizen of, statement of Johnston's force,	57, 58
Biddle, C. J. Colonel, commanding Brigade south of Bedford,	65
speech in Congress in regard to General Patterson,	116
Biddle, Craig Major, at affair at Falling Waters,	49
minutes of council at Martinsburg,	54
letter to Hon. F. P. Blair,	83
Blair, F. P. Hon., states that General Scott knew of Johnston's coming, before Bull Run,	79–83
states the despatch of General Patterson received,	79–83
Bull Run, Battle of, popular feeling about,	9
false theory as to loss of,	10
causes of defeat stated by General Richardson,	93
" " " " Heintzelman,	94
" " " " Franklin,	95
" " " " Wadsworth,	96
" " " " Slocum,	96

122　INDEX.

	PAGE
Bull Run, Battle of, causes of defeat stated by General Barry,	96, 97
" " " " Keyes,	98
" " " " Barnard,	98, 99
" " " " Griffin,	99, 100
" " " Colonel Davies,	101
" " " General D. Tyler,	102
" " " " A. Porter,	103
" " " " Ricketts,	104
" summary of,	105
Bunker Hill, Patterson advanced to,	70
reconnoissance sent out from,	70
Cadwalader, Geo. General, opinion on recall of Patterson's troops,	35
at council at Martinsburg,	52–55
report of, on Johnston's force,	59
Cameron, Simon Hon., Secretary of War, approves conduct of General Patterson,	17
Cavalry, Patterson's force, June 18th,	35
" " " 28th,	45
Johnston's " " "	45
Chambersburg, camp formed at,	31
Charlestown, Patterson proposes to move to,	67
" ordered there by General Scott,	68
" reports when he will go to,	70
" " what route he will take,	70
" " preparation for advance from,	76–112
time of troops expire at,	77–84
movement to, not a retreat,	84–112
Congress, debate in, regarding despatch of Patterson,	78–83
Covode, John Hon., false assertion regarding despatch,	79–82
Curtin, A. G. Governor, call upon, for troops, by Patterson,	28
promptness of response by,	29
organizes Pennsylvania Reserves,	30
Crosman, Colonel, Deputy Quartermaster-General, efforts to furnish transportation,	50
at council, Martinsburg,	52–54
opinion of Johnston's retreat,	57
Davies, T. A. Colonel, opinion of causes of defeat at Bull Run,	101
Falling Waters, engagement at,	47
" General Patterson's official report of,	47
Felton, S. M., patriotically furnishes steamboat,	27
Franklin, General, opinion of causes of defeat at Bull Run,	95
Gibson, Colonel, letter to General Patterson,	114
Gooch, D. W. Hon., false assertion regarding despatch of Patterson,	79–81

PAGE

Gordon, General, review of Patterson's campaign, ... 109–114
Griffin, Charles General, opinion of causes of defeat of Bull Run, . 99, 100

Halleck, Major-General, U. S. A., favorable criticism on Patterson's campaign, ... 39
Harper's Ferry, preparation to capture, ... 31
   instructions of General Scott regarding, . . 31, 32
   evacuated by rebel forces, ... 33
   Patterson's preparation to hold, ... 71
Heights, Maryland, examination of, by General Newton, . . 41
Heintzelman, General, opinion of causes of defeat of Bull Run, . 94
Hicks, Governor, assistance rendered by, ... 27
Hudson, Lieutenant, commands battery at Falling Waters, . . 48

Infantry, force of Patterson's June, 25th, ... 43–47
  " Johnston's " " 43–45
  " " July, ... 58–63
  " Patterson's " 63
Inquiry, Court of, asked for by General Patterson, . . . 13
   refused him, ... 15
Intrenchments at Winchester, ... 57–63
   plan of, by Captain Simpson, U. S.
   Top. Engineers, . . . 71

Jackson, "Stonewall" General, attacks Patterson at Falling Waters, 47
Johnston, Jos. E. General, not related to General Patterson, . . 21
   driven from Harper's Ferry, . . . 33
   pursuit of, by Patterson, ... 33
   pursuit stopped by orders of General-in-chief, 33, 34
   force of, June 28th, ... 43–45
   " July, ... 58–63
   plan to entrap Patterson, ... 56
   detained at Winchester by Patterson, . 70–77
   departure telegraphed to Washington, . 78
   arrival, effect of his, at Bull Run, . . 93–105

Keim, W. H. General, appointed by Governor of Pennsylvania, . 26
   in command at Chambersburg, . . . 31
   at council at Martinsburg, ... 52–55
   letter to General Patterson, . . . 107
Keyes, E. D. General, opinion on causes of defeat at Bull Run, . 98

Lackland, Mr., report of Johnston's force at Winchester, . 60
Leesburg, Patterson proposes to go to, ... 38
   advantage of position at, ... 38, 39
   opinion of General Halleck on position at, . . 39

McCall, G. A. General, letter of, regarding Pennsylvania border, 65
McClellan, General, forbidden to send reinforcements to Patterson, 35
   mentioned, ... 117

124 INDEX.

	PAGE
McDonald, Mr., statement of Johnston's force at Winchester,	59
McDowell, General, success of, announced,	72–77
movements of, unknown to Patterson,	74
Martinsburg, false position for Patterson,	40–55, 111
entered by Patterson's forces,	49
Patterson too far advanced at,	57
Narrative, summary of Patterson's,	85
Negley, Major-General, at council at Martinsburg,	52–55
report on Johnston's force at Winchester,	58
letter to General Patterson,	109
Newton, John Major-General, advises Patterson to ask for a Court of Inquiry,	12
examines Maryland Heights,	41
at affair at Falling Waters,	49
at council at Martinsburg,	51–55
at Harper's Ferry,	74, 76
opinion of Johnston's retreat,	57
Oakford, Colonel, letter to General Patterson,	108
Owens, Joshua T. Colonel, commands 24th Pennsylvania Volunteers,	115
Patterson, Robert General, honorably discharged,	9
application for Court of Inquiry,	12
receipt of application of, acknowledged,	15
Court of Inquiry refused,	15
conduct of, approved by Secretary and Assistant Secretary of War,	17
conduct of, approved by the President,	18
application through Senate for letters and orders,	19
false accusations against,	20, 21
questions furnished Committee on War by,	22
appointed Major-General of Pennsylvania troops,	26
placed in command of Department,	26
opens Annapolis route to Washington,	27
calls on Governor Curtin for 25,000 more troops,	28
call of, revoked by War Department,	29
asks to enlist three regiments for the war,	29
refused by War Department,	30
prepares to retake Harper's Ferry,	31
instructions to, of General Scott,	31, 32
crosses Potomac in pursuit of Johnston,	33
troops of, recalled by General Scott,	34, 35
censured by public for not pursuing,	36, 37

INDEX. 125

	PAGE
Patterson, Robert General, asks to change his line and go to Leesburg,	37
presents the advantages of that move,	38, 39, 66
proposes to drive enemy to Winchester,	42
force of June 25th,	43, 45, 47
asks for reinforcements,	46
crosses Potomac without them,	47
column attacked at Falling Waters,	47
official report of engagement,	47
enters Martinsburg,	49
orders advance on Winchester,	51
suspends order,	52
calls council of war on,	52
statement to,	53
force at Martinsburg,	63
less than General-in-chief intended,	63
probable result of a defeat,	64
desires to protect the Shenandoah Valley,	64
letter to Brigadier-General McCall,	64
inability on this line to hold Johnston,	66
proposes to go to Charlestown,	67
ordered to go there,	68
asks when he shall approach Winchester,	68
ordered to make demonstrations, Tuesday, July 16th,	68, 69
success of, in retaining Johnston,	70, 75
informs General-in-chief the day he will go to Charlestown,	70
warns of expiration of term of service of troops,	70, 84
goes to Charlestown by Bunker Hill,	70
makes reconnoissance from Bunker Hill,	70
prepares to hold Harper's Ferry,	71, 74
asks, "Shall I attack?"	73, 74
appeals to troops to remain,	74, 76, 113
reports arrival at Charlestown,	75
prepares to advance from,	76, 112
refusal of troops to remain,	77, 113
keeps Johnston at Winchester,	77
ignorant of McDowell's failure,	78
informs of Johnston's departure from Winchester,	78, 83
relieved by General Banks,	85
summary of Narrative,	85
remarks on testimony before Committee,	86
review of General Scott's statement,	89–93

126 INDEX.

	PAGE
Patterson, Robert General, allusion in Scott's Autobiography to Patterson's service in Mexico,	92
not "Chief" in Shenandoah Valley,	92
review of testimony about Battle of Bull Run,	93–105
gives causes of defeat at Bull Run,	105
letter to, from Major-General Geo. H. Thomas, U. S. A.,	106
letter to, from Major-Gen. W. H. Keim,	107
" " Col. Richard A. Oakford,	108
" " Major-Gen. J. S. Negley,	109
" " Brig.-Gen. G. H. Gordon,	109
" " " James Shields,	114
" " Colonel Gibson, U. S. A.,	114
resolutions regarding, of 24th Regiment Pennsylvania Volunteers,	115
resolutions regarding, of 15th Regiment Pennsylvania Volunteers,	116
service of, in War of 1812–15,	118
remarks in Congress regarding, by Hon. C. J. Biddle,	116
Patterson, Francis E. General, opens route through Baltimore,	27
Pennsylvania, Governor of, organizes Reserves,	30
Reserves, origin of,	30
volunteers, 11th regiment at Falling Waters,	48
" 15th and 24th regiments, resolutions of,	115, 116
" quota of, promptness in supplying,	25, 26
Perkins, Lieutenant, U. S. A., at affair at Falling Waters,	48
President, the, approves conduct of General Patterson,	18
protests against fighting at Bull Run till his force arrives,	79, 80
Price, R. Butler Major, at affair at Falling Waters,	49
Porter, Andrew Brigadier-General, on causes of defeat at Bull Run,	103
Porter, Fitz John Major-General, advises Patterson to ask for a Court of Inquiry,	12
at affair at Falling Waters,	49
opinion of Johnston's retreat,	57
Rankin, A. N., statement of artillery left by Johnston at Winchester,	62
Richardson, J. B. General, opinion on causes of defeat at Bull Run,	93, 94
Ricketts, General, opinion on causes of defeat at Bull Run,	104
Sanford, Major-Gen., expected with two guns and three regiments,	54
Scott, Lieut.-Gen., goes to Europe,	16
instructions to General Patterson,	31, 32
recalls artillery and cavalry of Patterson,	34, 35
forbids pursuit of Johnston,	35
transmits supposed plan of the rebels	56

INDEX.   127

	PAGE
Scott, Lieut.-Gen., statement of artillery left at Winchester,	61, 62
orders Patterson to Charlestown,	68
" " hold Johnston, July 16th,	68
informs Patterson of McDowell's success,	72, 77
asks Patterson if Johnston has stolen a march,	73
asked by Patterson, "Shall I attack?"	73, 74
informed of Johnston's departure by Patterson,	78, 82
warned of expiration of term of service of troops,	70, 84
review of Patterson's statement to Committee,	86, 88
knew of Johnston's departure from Winchester,	88
on General Patterson's character in Mexico,	92, 118
Scott, T. A. Hon., in favor of granting Court of Inquiry,	17
Senate, U. S., resolution asking for correspondence and orders of General Patterson,	19
resolution not complied with,	19, 20
Shenandoah, Valley of the, Patterson's efforts to protect,	64
difficulty of advancing in,	91
failure of other commanders to hold,	92
Sherman, John Hon., moves in Senate for orders and correspondence of Patterson,	19
on staff of General Patterson,	29
sent to Washington about Annapolis route,	27
reports refusal of War Department to enlist more troops,	29
opinion on recall of troops from Patterson,	36
informs General Patterson of injustice done him,	37
Shields, James General, letter to General Patterson,	114
Simpson, Captain, U. S. Top. Eng., at council at Martinsburg,	52, 55
plan of works at Winchester,	71
Slocum, H. W. General, opinion of defeat at Bull Run,	96
Stone, Colonel, joins General Patterson,	49
at council at Martinsburg,	52, 55
Thomas, Geo. H. Major-Gen., advises Patterson to demand Court of Inquiry,	11
at affair of Falling Waters,	48
at council of war at Martinsburg,	52
advises to go to Charlestown,	55
opinion of Johnston's retreat,	57
letter approving Patterson's campaign,	106
Times, New York Daily, article of General Halleck on art of war in,	39
Transportation, inadequacy of Patterson's,	49, 70
Tripler, Surgeon, at affair at Falling Waters,	49
Troop, Philadelphia City, at affair at Falling Waters,	48
Troops, call on Governor of Pennsylvania for 25,000 additional,	28
" revoked by War Department,	29

	PAGE
Troops, Patterson asks to enlist for the war,	29
enlistment of, refused,	30
recalled from Patterson when across the Potomac,	34, 35
opinion of General Cadwalader on recall of,	35
" Hon. John Sherman on recall of,	36
number of Federal, June 25,	43, 47
" rebel, "	43, 44
" " July,	57, 62
" Federal, "	63
expiration of term of service,	46, 85
appealed to by Patterson to remain,	74, 113
clothing of,	76, 110
refusal of, to remain,	77, 113
Tyler, Daniel General, opinion of causes of defeat at Bull Run,	102
Valley of Shenandoah, efforts of Patterson to protect,	64
difficulty of advancing in,	91
failure of other commanders to hold,	92
Wadsworth, James General, opinion of causes of defeat at Bull Run,	96
War, Committee on Conduct of, action of,	21
unfairness of mode of proceeding,	22
opinion of Congress upon it,	25
false statement of members of,	79
testimony before,	86
" as to Bull Run,	93
War, Council of, called by Patterson at Martinsburg,	52
minutes of,	54, 55
War, Secretary of, approves conduct of General Patterson,	17
declines to furnish orders to Senate,	19
Assistant, in favor of granting court,	17
Wellmore, Captain, statement of Johnston's force,	57, 58
Whiting, Major, plans defensive works at Winchester,	61
Winchester, Patterson proposes to drive enemy to,	42
orders an advance on,	51
" suspended,	52
intrenchments at,	57, 63
Johnston's forces detained there,	70, 77
his departure from, telegraphed by Patterson,	78
Wisconsin, 1st Regiment, Colonel Starkweather, at Falling Waters,	48
3d " at Harper's Ferry,	76

www.ingramcontent.com/pod-product-compliance
Lightning Source LLC
Chambersburg PA
CBHW022140160426
43197CB00009B/1364